VIGNETTES ON LIFE

2023
Dear Alisha and
Gerry,
Happy Chanukah!
With love,
Carol

VIGNETTES ON LIFE

*Reflections of a
Septuagenarian*

CAROL HARKAVY

Milan Book Publishing

First Printing, 2023
Milan Book Publishing

Also by Carol Harkavy

Rosie (and me) - a memoir

Readers' Five-Star Reviews

"After reading Rosie (and me), I was convinced that mothers are made from the same mold. The memoir is filled with ebullience and poignance. A pure, thorough and heartwarming journey of courage, love, vulnerability and comfort delicately woven to create a blanket of a masterpiece ready to nestle and provide warmth. I could perceive the life of my mother, so similar to the life of Rosie, yet born and lived miles apart." - Amazon Reviewer

"This is a story about unlimited family love. After reading the first page, I could not put the book down. After reading the last page, I wanted more! I know this book will always remain #1 in my extensive kindle library."- Amazon Reviewer

"The book was funny, and sad, honest and kind. It had great depth; touching memories and stories that invoked a physical response at times. I would chuckle out loud at silly things and cried towards the end."- Amazon Reviewer

"A very enjoyable journey into the relationship between a mother and daughter, this well-told memoir makes you feel as if you are right there sitting next to the author. It is a touching and satisfying read." - Amazon Reviewer

"A wonderful memoir, a tribute not only to a special relationship, but to the power of the English language to paint such a complex inspirational picture in so few words." - Amazon Reviewer

In memory of Steven Ratushewitz,

who missed out on all these years. . .

To Stefani Milan,
my good friend and fellow author, for her unwavering support,
encouragement, and most of all, her friendship.

Contents

PART SEVEN
WOMEN OF VALOR

PART EIGHT
WHAT WOULD ROSIE SAY?

"What's past is prologue."

William Shakespeare - *The Tempest*

vignette

(dictionary definition): a brief evocative description, account, or episode

(colloquial definition): a slice of life

Author's Note

You turn around, and suddenly there are seventy candles on your birthday cake! I am a member of a dying generation known as the Baby Boomers, created by the explosion of births after the Second World War. It was a generation filled with hope and optimism, following a period of war, uncertainty, and economic depression. Born in 1944, I am the proud progeny of the Greatest Generation. It was a tough act to follow.

As I approached my three-quarter of a century mark, I became more and more determined to write a memoir, *Vignettes on Life: Reflections of a Septuagenarian*. After perusing hundreds of my personal handwritten journal entries that spanned more than three decades, it became clear that I had the foundation for a memoir filled with life lessons that traversed not only time and place, but family dynamics, personal growth, and emotions as well.

Nelson Mandela's quote "It always seems impossible until it's done" reminds us that every one of our dreams can become a reality. At the age of seventy-three, after many years of procrastination, uncertainty, negativity, and self-doubt, I published my first memoir, *Rosie (and me)*. Having accomplished what once seemed impossible, I truly believe that I am in a position to urge others to recognize and overcome self-imposed obstacles before they thwart their ability to follow their passions.

It is my hope that this book of vignettes will impress upon my younger readers how important it is not to be late for the dance and to make my older readers aware that it is *never* too late to follow their hearts.

Mine has been an incredible journey, filled with peaks and valleys, joy and sorrow, self-doubt and self-actualization. Hang on tight! I hope you enjoy the ride!

Sincerely,
Carol Harkavy

Note: In order to keep my working title, I made every effort to complete this memoir before my 80th birthday!

(Readers: Please note the dates of the journal entries throughout this book of vignettes as it is important to understand their significance and meaning only in the context of the time in which they were written.)

PART ONE

Rearview Mirror

One

Resisting Technology
(Kicking and Screaming!)

Luddite: someone who is opposed or resistant to
new technologies or technological change

Nowhere is the contrast between a world consumed by advanced technology versus the benefits of leading a simple life more clearly illustrated than in George Orwell's *1984* and Henry David Thoreau's *Walden Pond*.

On June 8, 1949, George Orwell published his legendary polit-ical-social science fiction novel, *1984*. In it, he described a society not unlike the one we are currently experiencing more than seventy years later. With the year 1984 thirty-five years into the future, Orwell's concept seemed far-fetched and almost too fantastical to comprehend; but now it seems that his predictions have come to fruition. Terms like **Big Brother**, *newspeak*, *thought-crime*, and **doublethink** have become commonplace. Government intervention with its arbitrarily-imposed mandates as well as other repressive forces of governments and the media throughout much of the world have led to a totalitarianism that is nothing short of Orwellian.

Following the untimely death of his wife, George Orwell sequestered himself in a house on the remote Scottish island of Jura where he spent the next three years writing *1984*. He led a simple spartan existence without even the basic luxury of electricity, coping with the devastating effects of tuberculosis, to which he finally succumbed seven months after the publication of *1984*.

We are living in an age when Facebook, Instagram, Twitter, and YouTube, not to mention the government itself, have the technology to monitor our thoughts, identify all of our political and retail preferences, pinpoint our sexual predilections, know what kinds of games we like to play, what charities we support, what chocolate we prefer, and what coffee we like. Try as we might, there is no place to hide, no way to escape, nowhere to dodge the far-reaching tentacles of technology. It is *1984* in the flesh.

* * *

Over one hundred years before the publication of *1984*, Henry David Thoreau retreated to a small sparse cabin in a remote area of Concord, Massachusetts, where he wrote his masterpiece, **Walden Pond**. In it, Thoreau extols the benefits of living simply and taking the time to contemplate, walk in the woods, write, and reflect on nature. It is a philosophical treatise on simplifying one's life in order to achieve self-reliance and individualism.

Given the choice, I would seclude myself to a cabin on Walden Pond rather than a dwelling on an island off the coast of Scotland!

My journal entry of December 6, 2000 exemplifies my aversion to modern technology:

I heard over the radio the other day that they would like to do away with punch cards. This was in response to the year 2000 (often referred to as Y2K) election fiasco which will go down in history as one of the closest presidential races in the history of our country. It was in Florida that those assigned to tallying the voting cards were obsessed with hanging chads, illegible markings, and other discrepancies in the voting process. The dispute is over some five hundred votes by which George W. Bush is leading his opponent, Al Gore. Newspapers, legal briefs, and history books will explain the situation far better than I ever could, so suffice it to say, for the purpose of this entry, the IBM voting machines utilizing punch cards are under scrutiny.

I can remember when computers first became popular and becoming a key punch operator was all the rage. At that time, computers utilizing key punch cards were housed in several large temperature-controlled rooms, and what one small personal computer can do today in mere moments took several days to accomplish. I shock my children and grandchildren when I tell them that the inexpensive, simple handheld calculators they now take for granted cost close to three hundred dollars and were hard to come by when I was a teenager. Doris Day appeared in the 1962 movie, **That Touch of Mink***, where the machines go out of control, and thousands of punch cards fly wildly around the room that house several large computers. That scene reminds me of the hilarious* **I Love Lucy** *episode where Lucy and her friend Ethel are working in a candy factory assembly line, trying desperately, but unsuccessfully, to keep up with packaging the candies. As a result, they start to frantically pop as many candies into their mouths as possible. Both scenes epitomize technology gone amok.*

What I found incredible when I heard that machines using punch cards were now obsolete and would no longer be used is that I managed to be completely oblivious and uninvolved with an entire era of technology that was born, grew, flourished, and eventually became extinct.

Even though I had given some thought to learning how to enter that field of new technology, I never learned how to program the cards, run the machines, or how to collect, much less interpret, the data that these machines spit out. Even during the infancy stages of computer programming, I was much more interested in people-oriented jobs and, as a result, pursued a career in teaching. I have reflected on my lack of desire or inclination to learn about and utilize such technological advancement and have come to the conclusion that I love having a connection with humans and have no desire to have a relationship with machines. Perhaps it is a lame excuse for not taking the initiative or having the wherewithal to sit down and learn how to use modern technology. In that regard, I am the very definition of a luddite.

Despite shocked outcries by my contemporaries who have jumped on the technological bandwagon and claim that utilizing a computer would enhance my life, I strongly believe that the opposite is true. I prefer interactive behavior to the Internet. I would rather be surrounded by people than surf the Net. I like having a relationship with my mate instead of with my modem. Take me on a peaceful drive through quiet back roads, and you can stay plugged into your hard drive. Give me a walk in the country, hearing the birds sing, feeling the sunshine on my face, listening to a babbling brook, admiring nature, and you can keep your technology, along with your carpal tunnel syndrome from repetitive hand movements on the keyboard, your bad back from sitting in front of the computer for hours, and myopic vision from staring at a computer screen until you lose track of time.

I do not want to be thoroughly modern Millie. I like being an old-fashioned plain Jane. If I am still around when the personal computer has become obsolete, will I still rely on a pad and pen to express my surprise that an entire technological era of yet another half century has come and gone? Shall I allow simplicity to reign? Will I while away my time as amazing inventions become obsolete and momentous events go unnoticed? Will a yellow pad and a pencil only be available in an antique shop?

Two

The Good Old Days

Some people call them the good old days, but I prefer the age of innocence. They were the days of bobby socks, saddle shoes, white bucks, pink felt poodle skirts, and dancing the Lindy Hop to the tune of "Rock Around the Clock." Fifty years from now, the children of today will remember surgical masks, rubber gloves, virtual learning, and Zoom. How lucky I was to have grown up in an age where we could immerse ourselves in the innocence of youth, when we were not exposed to a deadly virus, social media rants, vitriolic political rivals, and cell phones connected to our ears with pods that look like cigarette butts.

We had been going to Spring Valley, New York, a small village in Rockland County thirty-five miles north of New York City, for many summers before we moved there permanently in 1955. My father had bought a cottage on Decatur Avenue in the small hamlet of Monsey when it was still part of Spring Valley and decades before it became an Orthodox Jewish enclave. It was there that my father's mother, my grandma Esther, taught us how to knit, interrupted only on *Shabbos* (the Jewish day of rest) or the times she had to inject herself with insulin to control her diabetes. We swam in Ellish Lake and played in the woods with the Salvaggi kids, all six of them, including Kathryn, who had Down syndrome. I sat in awe as Mrs. Salvaggi prepared her own margarine by adding yellow food coloring to a plastic bag filled with lard, kneading it together, resulting in an unhealthy spread that looked like butter. My widowed Aunt Sophie and her two daughters spent every summer with us in Spring Valley. Each morning, she commuted with my father to the dry cleaning store in New York City where they worked tirelessly in the toxic environment that would eventually kill them both. The carbon tetrachloride and perchloroethylene caught up with them some thirty-five years later when they both died within five years of each other, each with a different form of cancer. Aunt Sophie succumbed to lymphoma, and acute leukemia stole my father's life. They were both seventy-four.

When we moved to Spring Valley, there were only two elementary schools. One was at the north end of Main Street and the other was at the south end, so they were called North Main Street School and South Main Street School, respectively. The simplicity of the school names reflected life itself. I went to South Main Street School even though North Main Street School was closer to my home. State law proclaimed that you had to live at least two miles away in order to take the school bus. But my mother didn't drive; and because I lived closer than two miles away from North Main Street School, I was only entitled to school bussing if I went to South Main Street School which was situated more than two miles away. Government bureaucracy even then!

Television reception, by today's standards, was terrible. Snow covered the black-and-white screen and was often accompanied by rapid vertical motion of the image for no apparent reason. An outing to the movie theater in Spring Valley was a major event, not only because of the film that was playing, but mostly because the theater was air conditioned, a luxury very few people enjoyed in their homes. In fact, the marquee boasted **YOUR ALL NEW AIR-CONDITIONED SPRING VALLEY MOVIE THEATER**. Across the street was Brown's Ice Cream Parlor, where we spun on upholstered fountain stools, while sipping chocolate malteds and black-and-white (chocolate and vanilla) ice cream sodas.

It was such a treat to go to the movies that I was exhilarated one day when Aunt Sophie told us she would take us. When we ended up not going, I moped around all day, mumbling to myself, *"I knew it was too good to be true!"* What a disappointment for a six-year-old little girl. When she saw how upset I was, she cheered me up by putting pin-curls into my stick-straight hair to give me a beautiful wave.

During those long summer days, we passed the time playing *pisha-paysha* with our grandmother who taught us the old European card game she had learned as a child in Austria. She patiently showed us how to knit, and we spent hours knitting shrugs with bright multicolored Red-Heart yarn. In the afternoons while taking her afternoon nap, my mother, already stricken with her rheumatoid arthritis, kept us occupied by assigning us the task of picking up rocks. We whiled away the lazy summer days by listening to my sister Pearl's idol Johnny Ray singing "Mr. Sun" or "Your Cheatin' Heart" on the radio or laying out a blanket and reading under the shade of a tree. We were surrounded by woods, where we hiked and played and where my older siblings and cousins smoked my mother's cigarettes that they made me steal for them. How did we survive with a television that had just seven channels? What did we do without computers, iPads, or cell phones? Our telephone was connected to a party line, and occasionally we would entertain ourselves by eavesdropping on other people's juicy conversations and scandalous gossip or listening to bored housewives complain about their inattentive husbands and rowdy kids. Summers seemed to last forever. On rainy days, we played Monopoly, and when the weather permitted, we jumped rope or roller skated, played catch with our new pink Spaulding rubber balls, or ran around outside playing hide-and-seek or tag. We were always busy, managed to stay happy, and rarely complained about being bored.

Three

Going Back

November 5, 1992 *(journal entry)*

I have been experiencing recurrent dreams about my high school days, glorifying those days and longing for their return, often feeling tormented by the loss of that bygone era.

The dreams stopped abruptly after my twentieth high school reunion. It was then that I realized that I did not miss high school per se or the people or the experiences. What I really missed was that carefree period of my life when my time was my own, when the days flowed one into the other filled with a mundane routine of waking up early, going to school, meeting friends, talking to teachers, taking tests, eating lunch in the cafeteria (always with chocolate chip mint ice cream for dessert), coming home on the school bus, having a snack, relaxing, doing homework, eating dinner, studying for a test, watching television, being pampered by my mother - "Go relax, Ketzila (little kitten). I'll clean up the dishes." - going to sleep, and starting all over again the next morning. There was no mortgage payment to meet every month, no staying up all night with a sick child, no worrying about an elderly parent lying deathly ill in the hospital (on the day of my reunion, my father had just been diagnosed with acute leukemia, and it was only because of his insistence that I went to the reunion at all).

We can never go back nor should we try. My husband talks about what a fast runner he was when he was a kid, how he could read a book a day during his summer vacation, or go for long walks through the Bronx Zoo. I tell him we cannot go back. Those times have passed us by. They are simply memories.

Last night I dreamt about my best friend Janice. We lived in the same town and did everything together. We vacationed in Puerto Rico when we were nineteen, partied in Greenwich Village, shopped at the mall, ate dinner out, and went to the movies. I was her maid of honor, and she was mine. Regrettably, over the years, we lost contact, and when I was finally able to track her down in Florida, I found out that she had recently passed away.

In my dream, I was planning to visit Janice at her home on Francis Place, but I never got there. I encountered every possible obstacle preventing me from arriving at her house at the prearranged time of 10:00 p.m.

First, I took a nap, and I didn't wake up until after 11:00 p.m. When I started driving to her house, there was a detour that took me in the opposite direction from my destination. I went through Main Street and made a right up the hill, hoping to make another right turn to get back on the right road. But when I got to the top of the hill, there was a one-way sign going left instead of right. So I drove on, hoping to make my turn farther down the road, but every arrow was one way in the wrong direction. By this time, I was totally lost, so I went into Pakula's Bakery to ask for directions.

"Francis Place? Yes," said the young man in the store. "It's just up the street."

"Can I walk?" I asked hopefully.

"No. It's too far," was the response I did not want to hear.

The next thing I knew, I was swimming in a lake trying to get to Janice's house So now I was trying to swim to Janice's house, but there was a boat behind me trying to stop me. It was midnight. My arms hurt. I was tired of trying. I was totally exhausted. It was too late. And I knew I would never make it.

I woke up in a sweat and realized right then and there that we can **never** go back.

Four

On Time

"Time is too slow for those who wait,
Too swift for those who fear,
Too long for those who grieve,
Too short for those who rejoice,
But for those who love, time is eternity."

Henry Van Dyke-1904
(American author)

Unlike the lyrics in the song "Unchained Melody," where the Righteous Brothers declare that "time goes by so slowly," time actually goes by rather fast. There was a time up until not that long ago when I was saddened by how quickly time passed. But of late, I am no longer bothered by the speed at which time flies. Perhaps it is because I am truly content with this stage of my life. I used to find it unsettling that suddenly it was nine o'clock on a Sunday morning, and I was watching *Sunday Morning* on CBS yet again. What happened to the past week? How did Sunday morning arrive so soon? But now, in actuality, it is rather comforting to know that I have lived to see yet one more Sunday morning.

When I was a child, the concept of time was pretty vague. Summers seemed to last forever, and tomorrow referred to any time that was after today! I see it with my grandchildren. They never lament about how quickly another week has passed or how soon their birthdays come around. Time is not something that they dwell upon, and every day brings new joy filled with brand-new adventures.

They say that as we get older, we revert back to our childhood. Perhaps that is what is happening to me. I can sleep late if I want; I can exercise, read, walk, or write whenever I want; I can do chores or not depending on my mood. Basically, I can do what I want whenever I want. After decades of rushing around, meeting deadlines, working constantly, dealing with payrolls and insurance companies, making mortgage payments on time, paying a bottomless pile of bills, getting our children through college and launched into their adult lives, and fulfilling other seemingly endless obligations, I can finally sit back, relax, and smell the roses. I have the luxury of being able to take the time to appreciate every miracle surrounding me - the sun, the breeze, the smiles on my grandchildren's faces as they look with wonder on things that I have, for so long, taken for granted.

My brother Siggy got an autograph album when he graduated from junior high school. In the back of the album were some sample entries. At the tender age of eight, I chose this one:

> *"Yesterday is gone. Forget it!*
> *Tomorrow has not come. Don't worry.*
> *Today is here. Use it!"*

Happily, I am now enjoying the todays of my life.

Five

Thoughts Around Birthday Time

(For this vignette, I have chosen a few of the journal entries I made around the time of my birthday. If I included them all, this vignette alone would take up an entire book!)

June 15, 1991 **(journal entry)**

      I am almost forty-seven years old, and for as long as I can remember, I have been a facilitator, always striving for harmony and tranquility. I need things to go smoothly - no waves, no unpleasant encounters, no strained relationships, no rocking the boat.
      *I have often likened myself to the main character in the play, **Death of a Salesman,** where Willy Loman states emphatically that he does not want to be liked, but **well**-liked. Perhaps this has been the driving force behind my unending addiction to facilitation, forever trying to please*

others. *It is only recently that I realize the wisdom of my aunt Sarah's advice when she told me a long time ago, "If you try to please everyone, you end up pleasing no one, especially not yourself."*

* * *

June 25, 1996 (journal entry)
Allendale, NJ

Today is my birthday! Simple math reveals that I am fifty-two years old. In an effort at humor, I tell people that I am twenty-five, reversing the two digits of my age!

I got up at 6:30 a.m. to have breakfast with Emily, my twenty-one-year-old "baby," who is an intern at a medical publishing company in New York City. We bond at the local 1950s luncheonette three mornings a week before she boards the train from Allendale to New York. After Emily leaves, I remain seated at the vintage chrome and formica table, reminiscing about my life twenty-five years ago.

Twenty-five years ago! Where was I? What were my dreams? What was I doing? What were my hopes? What were my aspirations?

It was 1971. My oldest son Todd was two years old, and I was pregnant with Jeffrey who would not be born for another month and a half. We were living at 334 East 108th Street between 1st and 2nd Avenues in Spanish Harlem, three blocks north and five blocks east of New York Medical College where Steve, my husband of five years, was completing his third year. We had been living there for three years and had the best neighbors we ever had before or since that time. Mr. Mays, the resident guard of our building, was always standing outside the front door, watching the comings and goings of the tenants, making sure that no one who didn't belong passed by him. Built like a linebacker, no one messed with Mr. Mays! And there was Miss Francis, my eighty-year-old upstairs neighbor with whom I conversed during our climb up fourteen flights of stairs because the elevator was out of order. I was eight months pregnant, and while climbing the stairs, she told me that she wished that just **one** man would have a baby so that the whole world would know what it was like to give birth! A precocious six-year-old child named Effie lived next door. Her father taught me how to stop Todd's hiccups by wetting a piece of a brown paper bag and putting it on his forehead. There was Mr. Prenz, the janitor, always pleasant and friendly, who called me out of the elevator one day because he did not recognize or trust the person following me. Peggy, our nanny, robust and energetic at forty-five, had been taking care of Todd for the past ten months. My father, still working at the New York State Unemployment Office in his hometown of Spring Valley, New York, was a young sixty-one; and my mother, her body not yet totally ravaged by the arthritis that had plagued her for the past thirty years, was fifty-eight and looking forward to the arrival of my second baby and her eighth grandchild. It was a time of working hard and dreaming of an exciting future, an interim period between where we were and where we were going, always striving to do better.

I was teaching in the Speech Department of City College (my alma mater), working with my old professors - where Helen . . . .

* * *

January 4, 1997 **(journal entry)**

(aside) It is now six-and-a-half months since I began writing the previous journal entry. I did not even complete the sentence I was writing! Did the phone ring? Was I late for work? Did I suddenly realize I had to pay a past-due bill? Obviously, whatever it was that was so important for me to interrupt my writing in the middle of a sentence has long since been forgotten and has totally escaped my mind. This entire scenario is a reflection of my life. I have become totally consumed by my required mundane daily activities that constantly take precedence over the things

I would prefer to do, such as following a healthy exercise routine, taking walks, interacting more with my children, and, yes, writing my memoirs.

I returned to my journal today, hoping to pick up where I left off seven months ago when I left poor Helen hanging in mid-sentence! Alas, because it is almost impossible to recapture a moment once it is lost, I never did go back to reconstructing my life twenty-five years earlier.

I am reminded of a quote by Robert Burns. "The best laid plans of mice and men often go awry." Or as my husband Steve says, "Life interferes with life."

* * *

June 25, 1999 *(journal entry)*
Bergenfield, NJ

The day before my fifty-fifth birthday, I bought $171 worth of lotions, creams, and soaps at the new bath shop called "Bathing Beauties" in Ramsey, New Jersey.

My best friend Avis met me later in the day and took me out for lunch at the Ho-Ho-Kus Inn. It is always such a relaxing and peaceful time for both Avis and me when we get together. Life slows down while we reminisce and talk about our families, our concerns, our daily lives, and our innermost feelings. It is hard to believe that Steve met Avis' husband John on the first day of medical school over thirty years ago. John was single then, while Steve and I had been married for all of two years. Later in the year, when I was quite obviously pregnant with our first child, we went to meet John's mother, a petite perky devout Catholic. When John introduced me to his mother as his girlfriend, she looked in horror at my rather large belly, then at John, and then back at me, until we finally told her it was only a joke. I really wasn't John's new pregnant Jewish girlfriend, and, with a huge sigh of relief, Nellie was able to put down her rosary beads!

John's real girlfriend was Avis, whom I did not meet until their wedding in June of 1969. We immediately became fast and close friends, married to two Type A personality, loyal, and loving overachievers. We had a lot in common. We lived near the medical school; we were both teachers; and our easygoing accommodating personalities allowed our marriages to medical students to flourish while others were failing. We overlooked much of the stress and hard work that went with the territory of being married to a medical student. We became part of each other's families; we fished in the waters off Montauk; we stayed at bed-and-breakfasts in New York and Connecticut; we formed the Married Couples Club at New York Medical College; we confided in each other and shared our feelings and our hopes for the future. And now, thirty years later, we still commiserate and reminisce. There is no pretense, no bullshit, no airs, no jealousy - just genuine love and companionship.

During our lunch, Avis gave me my birthday present - a bag filled with bath soaps, oils, and creams. And that night, Steve gave me his birthday present - a large box filled with Crabtree and Evelyn body lotion, soaps, powder, and bath wash. What is there about middle age that screams for rejuvenating body creams and lotions? I suppose, like Fisher-Price toys are age-appropriate for preschoolers and Healthtex matching outfits are geared toward young children, lotions and creams are designed to target middle-aged women.

* * *

June 25, 2001 **(journal entry)**
Bergenfield, NJ

The craving is insatiable. I don't know how to satisfy it. I consume four cups of coffee, three slices of bread with apricot preserves, and even a piece of the forbidden halavah, so high in fat and sugar. But nothing helps. I sit outside. I try to read. I work. I rearrange closets. I clean the house and dust the furniture. *Nothing is satisfying. Nothing can fill the emptiness I feel. And then it becomes clear. I need her. I want her.*

For fifty-six years, she has wished me a happy birthday, and this will be my first birthday ever without her, the first time I won't hear her lovely familiar off-key rendition of "Happy Birthday," always the first call on the morning of my birthday.

Sometimes, when I bemoan how much I miss my mother, I feel very selfish. Women I know personally have lost their mothers at much younger ages. Some were young adults, others were only children. I consider myself very fortunate to have had her for so many years. How many grandmothers, like me, still have their mothers around to link the generations and exchange ideas about what was then and what is now? But it does not diminish how much I miss her and wish she were here to wish her baby, her *ketzila*, a happy birthday.

* * *

June 25, 2004 **(journal entry)**

I wander aimlessly into **The Gem Mine**, an upscale jewelry consignment shop in Westwood, New Jersey, where the petite, pert, gray-haired proprietor Mary, greets me with, "Carol, what's wrong? You seem down." It is true. I am usually bright and bubbly, always with a smile, but this day I am sluggish and glum. "Oh, Mary," I moan. "Today is my 60th birthday," I announce forlornly.

"Sixty!" Mary chortles, waving her hand. "Sixty is easy! **Seventy** is tough!"

So I cheered up and bought myself an ivory and amber necklace.

* * *

June 25, 2008 *(journal entry)*
Haddonfield, NJ

On this, my sixty-fourth birthday, I am sitting at the dining room table in the lovely condo we have been renting in Haddonfield, New Jersey, for the past year. I soak in the array of photos I have hanging on the wall. I smile at my baby picture taken when I was three months old, holding my chubby little feet that are now a size 10! My eyes travel over to my parents' wedding photo, a collage of various poses of my paternal grandmother looking considerably older than her fifty years, my uncle Hymie's diploma from The Brooklyn College of Pharmacy dated May 11, 1916, my mother-in-law's formal engagement portrait, boyhood pictures of my father, snapshots of Steve's paternal grandparents and his maternal grandmother, as well as a photograph of his parents taken in Atlantic City on their honeymoon. I peer out through the French doors and admire the beautiful sunrise. In front of the doors is the antique birdcage I displayed on the new sunporch of our first house in 1974. It is filled with live plants and a collection of carved parrots.

Like a young child, I woke up in the middle of the night in happy anticipation of my birthday. I saw the full moon from my bedroom window, heard the birds singing outside, listened to the soft snoring and steady breathing of my partner and love of my life sleeping next to me, and gave thanks to God for having awakened to welcome yet another birthday.

At sixty-four years old, my stomach sags, there is more salt in my hair than there is pepper, spider veins have popped out on my legs, and three liver spots seem to have materialized overnight on the back of my right hand. I laugh too loudly and my smile is too wide, accentuating my overbite. My once firm and defined neck and chin are now wrinkled, and crow's feet have emerged around my eyes. But even though I have lost some stamina and flexibility, I consider myself blessed to have found peace, comfort, and tranquility as I approach the late autumn of my life.

I have already outlived my maternal grandmother Fanny by

a year. I was six years old when she died, and she seemed so old to me! I suppose I look very old to my own grandchildren. My paternal grandmother Esther lived to seventy-four, as did my father; and my mother Rosie surprised everyone by making it to eighty-seven.

* * *

June 24, 2009 *(journal entry)*
Grindhouse Cafe
Haddonfield, NJ

"It's amazing how old we've gotten," I lament to my cousin, Cecile, on her birthday, just two days before mine.

"And so fast!" she replies without missing a beat. Cecile is exactly four years and two days older than I. She just turned sixty-nine, and I will be an official senior citizen tomorrow. Being the baby in my family has always made me feel forever young, so the number "65" is hard to fathom, but I'll get used to it!

*Despite my gratitude for reaching this milestone, it definitely feels very strange turning sixty-five as I wander around the wonderful town with brick sidewalks, Victorian homes, shops, and coffeehouses that Steve and I have called "home" for the past two years. This morning, I even enjoyed folding clothes, clothes smelling so fresh and clean, reminding me of the young girl named Emily in **Our Town** who just w....*

* * *

July 1, 2009 - 7:30 a.m. *(journal entry)* - a week later
Haddonfield, NJ

*Wow! That was a first! Stopping in the middle of a **word**, for goodness' sake! I've stopped in the middle of a thought - even a sentence -*

but stopping in the middle of a word. Now that takes the cake! First, let me finish the word, the sentence, and the thought, and then I'll attempt to provide an explanation for the abrupt halt in finishing the word. (Back to **Our Town**). . . where Emily just wanted to come back to earth for one more day - "to clocks ticking....and Mama's sunflowers. And food and coffee. And new ironed dresses and hot baths....and sleeping and waking up." What a blessing it is to wake up in the morning, having the strength and wherewithal to wash and dry your own laundry and then to enjoy the fresh clean smell as it is removed from the dryer (the clothesline is even better - but that is a memory from long ago - clothespins and lines and the fire escape on 16th Street in New York City where my mother stood to hang the washed clothes). If only we could always see the wonder of the world through the eyes of my three-year-old granddaughter, Becky. She relishes in the wonder of the rain, a puddle, the jolt of the elevator when it starts to ascend, the thrill of being able to reach the elevator button for our floor, the excitement of trying on Crocs, of going to the Blueberry Festival (or as she calls it, "The Bluebelly Festival"), of getting a balloon and a Dora the Explorer shirt. To recapture the wonder of even the most mundane things around us is truly a blessing. Lately, over the past couple of years, when the hustle and bustle of work and motherhood have finally faded into the past and time has become so deliciously available, I have been able to enjoy the most valuable commodity one can have - the luxury of time. I thank God daily for being here, for being alive, and for being in good health. So, although the novelty of the rain, the thunder, the breezes, and even the smell of clean sheets has passed, I still enjoy the wonder of it all, and I am so grateful for the gift of having the time to embrace all of the miracles surrounding me.

I couldn't figure out what had abruptly prevented me from completing a word in the journal entry commemorating my 65th birthday. Maybe it was a series of phone calls from loved ones wishing me a happy birthday, or perhaps the dryer had stopped and I felt compelled to attend to the clothes. Whatever it was, I doubt that it merited such a sudden interruption of my writing.

Now, six days into my sixty-fifth year, I am enjoying the dawn of a new day, sitting at a wrought-iron table outside of the Grindhouse Cafe in Haddonfield and marveling at the flowers being watered by public works men from the back of their municipal pick-up truck as they reach the tops of the hanging baskets with long hoses. I have arrived at the point where I selfishly enjoy the simple things in life - the charm of our small town or going to see the 3-D movie **Up** with Emily and her family, smiling at Becky wearing her oversized 3-D glasses, her thumb in her mouth, reaching for some more Skittles to nosh on after polishing off her Cracker Jacks.

"Selfish" is not a word I generally use to describe myself. But now I adamantly guard my sense of inner peace and equanimity. I have worked hard, sacrificed much time and effort in raising my children and working with my husband toward our common goals. Now, it is my time to use as selfishly as I wish. And I don't mean fancy vacations, luxury hotels, or expensive restaurants. Been there, done that. I mean just the simple things in life. These feelings were suppressed for a very long time; but then all of a sudden I turn around - and BOOM! I'm sixty-five, and I long for the time I no longer have. If I could do it all over again, I would take more time to smell the roses. It's funny, but at the time I thought I did. I certainly loved seeing my children grow up and happily experienced each and every milestone. We took regular vacations instead of waiting for some indefinite time in the future. I enjoyed my interactions with our patients in the office and felt satisfaction in helping them. But if this **were** a dress rehearsal and I could do it again, I would make sure I made more time for myself. That brings me to the here and now, the only time of which I am certain. In **Les Miserables**, the girl sings of a time gone by "when dreams were made and used and wasted." So I will enjoy the time I have, use it wisely, and try not to waste it.

June 25, 2011 *(journal entry)*

My granddaughter, Becky, isn't happy about my age. She feels that sixty-seven is too old.

"You're almost one hundred!" bellowed little "Becky aig 5" (as she signed her card to me, misspelling "age" and wishing me a happy birthday). She counted from sixty-five to ninety-five and then announced sadly, "When you're one hundred, you die!"

What a wake-up call!

* * *

June 25, 2018 *(journal entry)*
Cherry Hill, NJ

Turning seventy-four years old this year is bittersweet for me. I always dreaded the thought of reaching this age. My father died at the age of seventy-four. So did his mother (my grandma Esther), as well as his sister, Sophie. A year and a half ago, my sister-in-law Susan died eight months after turning seventy-four. So that age has been the "witching hour" for me, and I cannot help associating turning seventy-four with dying. It reminds me of another superstition I held for a long time. I never memorized the Mourner's **Kaddish** (Hebrew prayer for the dead) when I was a young woman and my parents were still alive. I was afraid it would jinx their well-being. To this day (thirty-four years after my father died and seventeen years after my mother's death), I still cannot recite the **Kaddish**. But unlike refusing to learn the Mourner's **Kaddish**, I cannot avoid becoming seventy-four. (Well, I suppose I can, but I don't want to go there!)

I am hoping that my fear that this will be **the** year is not the cause of my despondency. But starting today, I will reframe and not waste a precious moment. I will try to be more productive and stop *being so disgusted with my inertia in writing, laxity in following my diet, procrastination in editing my audiobook, and resignation that this will be my final year. I refuse to waste this year just in case (I'll bite my tongue) it is my last.*

* * *

June 25, 2019 - 8:00 a.m. **(journal entry)**
Starbucks
Cherry Hill, New Jersey

Whew! I am still here! I survived seventy-four unscathed! I made it to seventy-five.

I walked down the winding path from my condo to Star-bucks (because I could), ordered a venti cappuccino (compliments of my Starbucks "birthday reward"), and am writing in my journal, all because I still can!

Three birthdays ago, **Rosie (and me)** *was just a gleam in my eye - a dream that I hoped would someday come true. Two birthdays ago, I was pumped up because* **Rosie** *had just been published a month before my birthday and nine days before Mother's Day. My last birthday found me in the throes of recording* **Rosie** *for an audiobook with my son, Jeff.*

So what have I learned in my almost - whoops! - in my actual three-quarters of a century? (Am I talking about me? It must be someone else!)

I try not to let things get to me. Tiny twinges in my left arm no longer trigger fears of a heart attack. Needing to lose the fifteen pounds I gained over the past three years is not terribly important in the scheme of things. Skipping days, even weeks, writing in my journal is not the end of the world. I have learned to pick my battles and not to sweat the small stuff. Bickering is silly. This reminds me of a cute story.

Steve and I took Aviva and her friend, Shanee, to the aquarium.

On the way home, I was bickering with Steve about which road to take. After listening to our sparring back and forth, Shanee leaned over to Aviva and whispered, "I love it when old people fight. They're *so* cute!"

That made us all laugh. Now, to be clear, Steve thinks there were three girls in the back seat - there were only two; and he believes we were arguing over where to park - we were actually on our way home. But it doesn't pay to argue over nonsense, and it is important to let things that are not positive and/or beneficial to our well-being roll off our backs. That is the place I strive to be.

So I look back on this past year, and I am truly grateful. I have three children, each happy doing their own thing, and I am blessed with thirteen wonderful grandchildren. Like my mother Rosie used to say, "The children are your investment, and the grandchildren are the dividends on that investment." Steve and I just celebrated fifty-three years of marriage; we have a roof over our heads; I am in relatively good health (took a three-mile hike with six other "seniors" and didn't slip and fall on the muddy slope like two of them did); I have published a book; I am nearer than further to finishing an audiobook; I have several book club presentations under my belt; I have a good relationship with my siblings; and I have as many friends as I can handle (not too many - okay, only one really good friend, Avis!).

I have learned to be more accepting of my modus operandi, warts and all; and I try to follow the advice written in 1932 by Reihhold Neibuhr (theologian) that became the motto for Alcoholics Anonymous:

God grant me -
The serenity to accept the things I cannot change.
The courage to change the things I can.
And the wisdom to know the difference.

Wait! What's all this talk about turning seventy-five? Being a

grandmother? Having thirteen grandchildren? Who am I talking about?
Oh, yes! It's me! Today is my birthday. Seventy-five, here I come!

Six

Growing Old

December 25, 1992 **(journal entry)**
South Beach, Florida

The old woman skillfully dodges the gaze of the young woman who is renting out beach chairs. She surreptitiously sits on a vacant chair, and as soon as she spots the cute young woman approaching, clipboard in hand, the wrinkled woman who has been overexposed to the intense Miami Beach sun, walks five feet away, lays down her towel on the sand and places her body, face down, on top of the towel. Out of the corner of her eye, she spots the "enemy," and when the young woman is out of her visual range, the old woman gets up, furtively heads toward the chair, only to find a young man lying there - another interloper who is also dodging the fangs of the chair monitor. I am tempted to pay the four dollars for the old woman to have a chair of her own without worry, but she indignantly tells the young man that the chair is hers, and he reluctantly goes on his way!

(Why do I see a metaphor here? Does the old woman represent old age; the beach chair, life; the young man, youth; and the enforcer of the beach chairs, death? Just asking.)

* * *

My sister Pearl took a philosophy class in college. I was eleven years old when she posed the following philosophical question to me: *What if this were all a dream, and you are really an old grandmother dreaming of your childhood?* For many years that concept gnawed at me. But guess what? Now I *am* that old grandmother! Or am I still that wide-eyed eleven-year-old, and this is all a dream?

* * *

My uncle Hymie, who lived to the age of ninety-eight, told me a story about meeting an old man who complained that he couldn't pee. Uncle Hymie asked him, "How old are you?" The man replied, "I'm ninety-five years old," to which Uncle Hymie retorted, "Then you peed enough already!"

At seventy-five, I have decided to apply Uncle Hymie's advice to my obsession with worrying. I've been worrying for seventy-five years. I've worried enough already!

* * *

Yesterday I was driving behind a Bentley automobile with handicapped license plates. The driver had obviously made it big in this world. He had "arrived," but not unscathed, as evidenced by the handicapped plates. The familiar Pennsylvania Dutch saying came to mind, **"We get too soon old and too late smart!"** Such is the story of life.

In the parking lot at Wegmans supermarket, an elderly man was struggling to gain his balance after getting out of his car. I asked him if he would like a cart to lean on, and he appreciatively answered, "Yes." He straightened himself up, leaned on the handle, placed his cane in the cart, and walked into Wegmans.

So many children and young adults think that old and frail people have always been that way. When my eleven-year-old granddaughter saw a photograph of her grandfather with thick black hair and a youthfulness that belies the current countenance of her Poppy, Aviva cried, "That's not Poppy. That's some young guy!"

The same goes for pictures of my mother in a wheelchair, looking blankly into the camera because of her blindness from macular degeneration. It is hard to imagine her as the vibrant, young, bright-eyed, energetic mother I remember with her almost eagle-eye vision, threading a needle, crocheting an intricate doily, or painstakingly removing a splinter from my hand with precision and ease.

I wonder about the man leaning on the Wegmans cart. Had he been an athlete or a professional businessman? Perhaps he was a college professor or an executive of a large corporation. We should try to visualize people as they might have been in the prime of their lives, rather than view them only as the aged, enfeebled folks they have inevitably become.

* * *

In 1961, I read George Orwell's book *1984*. It had been published in 1949, and at that time, 1984 was a year far into the future. Now it seems like ancient history.

* * *

Even young people grow wiser with age. I am reminded of a quote by Mark Twain, reflecting on his relationship with his father:

"When I was a boy of fourteen, my father was so ignorant I could hardly stand to have the old man around. But when I got to be twenty-one, I was astonished at how much the old man had learned in seven years."

* * *

When I was in my mid-sixties, I bought Judith Viorst's *I'm Too Young to Be Seventy: and Other Delusions* at a book sale for a buck. Seventy seemed pretty far away, and skimming through it then was not nearly as meaningful as reading it word by word now that I am in the middle of my seventh decade. The book is sitting snugly in my bookcase, joining Viorst's other books on age that I read religiously as I entered each decade of my life: **When Did I Stop Being Twenty: and Other Injustices, It's Hard to Be Hip Over Thirty: and Other Tragedies of Married Life, How Did I get to be 40: and Other Atrocities, Forever Fifty: and Other Negotiations, Suddenly Sixty: and Other Shocks of Later Life.**

It's funny to think that my life can be summed up in the flippant short books of Judith Viorst!

* * *

October 11, 2008 (*erev* - "eve before" - Yom Kippur) *(journal entry)*

When I was a much younger woman, I used to be bothered by how much of this world I would never experience. I agonized over the fact that there were so many people that I could never know, so many places that I would never visit, so many adventures I would never have. Now, I realize that my life is complete in the microcosm - the small part of the universe where I have found my niche. I am very content with my daily walks, weekly choir rehearsals, monthly local theater productions, occasional visits to Atlantic City, spontaneous phone calls from my grandchildren, quiet moments with my husband who has been the love of my life for over fifty years, reading and writing, doing yoga, tai chi, pilates and water aerobics, and even playing online poker.

It has become abundantly clear to me that I don't have to meet every last person out there to make sure that I have chosen the right ones in my life; I don't need to visit every corner of the world to convince myself that I have picked the best place to live; and it is not necessary to try to experience everything possible in order to feel fulfilled. I have traveled; I have raised a family; I have maintained a household as the sole breadwinner; I have given and received unbridled love to and from my parents and maintained an undying love for my husband. I have been charitable and felt loving-kindness for my fellow human beings. I have been spiritual in my approach to life and have asked to be forgiven for any behavior I regret and have forgiven those whom I think have wronged me. I have helped people in need, and I have tried to the best of my ability to right wrongs that I find unacceptable.

So, without tasting the entire world's palette, I am perfectly content living my life to its fullest in my own small corner of the universe.

Seven

Reflections

. . . . on smells

September 19, 1989 *(journal entry)*

Smells are so nostalgic! The fresh, earthy, ambrosial fragrance of early spring brings back wonderful memories of childhood, when I could go out with only a light sweater, roller skate up and down the sidewalk along 16th Street in New York City, or ride my Schwinn bike with no gears all around the property in Spring Valley.

Latex paint still makes me feel nauseated. In 1968, when Steve started medical school, we painted our new apartment in East Harlem with latex paint. I couldn't believe how nauseous I felt from the paint. I had always helped my father paint and never felt sick. But I was wrong. It wasn't from the paint that I felt ill. I was pregnant!

My mother's lipsticks had a strong, sweet, perfume smell. They were always the dark red that was the rage in the late 1940s and early 1950s. The clean sweet smell of baby powder makes me feel maternal, and it is hard to describe the delicious aroma of a baby's clean hair on a warm day. The combination of shampoo and perspiration is truly intoxicating.

Then there are unpleasant smells that are ominous and foreboding. The spearmint odor of the disinfectant used in hospitals harshly reminds me of my father's final days when his hospital room was kept sterile with the noxious-smelling disinfecting cleaner.

* * *

. . . .*on sound*

One day, when I was talking to a student in my office in the Speech Department at City College, I heard someone in the hall call out, "Carol, is that you?" I looked down the hallway and saw a blind young man walking with his white cane and seeing-eye dog.

Six years earlier, we were both students at the same college, and I volunteered to read his textbooks to him while a tape recorder was running so he could listen to the tape recording anytime he chose. There were no audiobooks available back then, so he relied on my recordings. What a coincidence that the blind man in the hall outside my office had been that student in the early 1960s to whom I had read over the course of a year. No wonder he recognized my voice. He heard it repeatedly when he studied history, literature, physics, and chemistry.

Eight

◎⬥◎

Rearview Mirror

The warning *Caution. Objects are closer than they appear* etched into the side-view mirrors of most automobiles is a metaphor of life itself.

It is true. Everything we look forward to soon becomes a thing of the past. For a major part of my life, the rapidity of time made me feel anxious. Days, weeks, months, and years seemed to fly by. In the last few years, though, I have developed an almost Zen-like attitude toward time. I am fortunate to have enjoyed a full life, never having to suffer the pains of chronic illness or financial ruin. I view each day as a gift, and no matter how much or little I do in any one day, I am grateful to have experienced that day at all. A ninety-five-year-old man once told me that whenever he wakes up on this side of the grass, it's a good day!

I like to observe young people talking, especially when it concerns their work, their future, their aspirations, and their dreams. I find their goals reminiscent of Steve's and mine so many years ago. Medical school, specialty boards, having a family, getting tenure, buying a house - all were hopes for the future. And now, not in a morbid way, all of those things can only be seen in that rear-view mirror. At the time, our dreams seemed very far away, almost unattainable; but in reality, like the cautionary sign etched in the side-view mirror reminds us, those objects were far closer than they appeared.

One of the joys of growing older is the luxury of revisiting one's life via the rearview mirror.

PART TWO

The Road Not Taken

One

On Fate

"A person often meets his destiny on the road he took to avoid it."
Jean de La Fontaine
(17th century poet)

After retiring as a civil engineer, my brother-in-law, Lenny Ra-tushewitz, wrote a book entitled **Things Happen.** It is a collection of short stories, each based on the significance of timing. *He woke up late, so he wasn't involved in the deadly accident that he witnessed just ahead of him while driving to work,* or *She decided to get to the bank early, and thus found herself the victim of an armed robbery.* I am reminded of the stories after the terror attack of 9/11, when people who were not supposed to report to work at the World Trade Center had switched days with a coworker; or a woman who was to start a new job on the 101st floor that day had to stay home because her baby-sitter got sick; or the lucky man whose alarm clock didn't go off, causing him to oversleep on that fateful morning.

July 9, 2011 *(journal entry)*
Starbucks
Haddonfield, NJ

 A freak accident happened two days ago at a Texas Rangers baseball game. A thirty-nine-year-old firefighter, who traveled an hour and a half with his young son to see the game, fell to his death while trying to catch a ball thrown to him by a player. The ball was foul, and in a magnanimous gesture, the player tossed the ball to the fan. While reaching for the ball, the young father toppled over the railing and crashed to his death twenty feet below. Lenny's book, **Things Happen***, came immediately to mind. What if the opposing team member hadn't hit a foul ball - what if it had been fair? What if the victim had bought cheaper seats and was not sitting so close to the players; or what if he had to work at the firehouse that day? What if the player decided to throw the ball into the sideline or ignored it altogether? What if the six-year-old, now without a father, had awakened with a fever or a stomachache or if they had decided to go to an amusement park instead of the game? We have so many choices in our lives, for which we either suffer the consequences or reap the benefits. All we can do is plan the best we can and hope for a good outcome.*

* * *

July 15, 2012 *(journal entry)*
Starbucks
Cherry Hill, NJ

 On July 4th, three children died in a boating mishap off the coast of Oyster Bay on Long Island when an overcrowded yacht capsized, trapping the three young passengers in the cabin. Whenever I hear tragedies like this, I often wonder about the scenario preceding the tragic event. I can picture the buzz and excitement in the household getting ready for the special day and the thrill the children felt because they could indeed go to see the fireworks from the water, promising to be good and to listen to their parents and to be careful. I envision the packing of snacks and drinks, making sure to wear a jacket or a sweater because it might be cold on the water. Short of a crystal ball, no one could have imagined that this promising happy outing would result in such a horrible tragedy.

* * *

A few days later, the eleven-year-old son of a pop singer was floating on an inner tube in a lake when he was hit by a Jet Ski. The child is brain dead. What scenario might have preceded this tragedy? What could have been safer than floating on a serene lake on a lazy hot summer day? Had the boy wanted to go hiking? Perhaps, his mother said, "No, no. That's too dangerous. You might fall and break your leg. There may be rattlesnakes in the woods. Better just hang out in your inner tube on the lake where it is safe."

We never know when we will get hit by the proverbial lightning. We just never know.

The Appointment in Samarra
(as retold by W. Somerset Maugham -1933)

DEATH SPEAKS:

There was a merchant in Baghdad who sent his servant to the market to buy provisions, and in a little while, the servant came back, white and trembling and said, "Master, just now when I was in the market-place I was jostled by a woman in the crowd, and when I turned, I saw it was Death that jostled me. She looked at me and made a threatening gesture; now, lend me your horse, and I will ride away from this city and avoid my fate. I will go to Samarra, and there Death will not find me."

The merchant lent him his horse, and the servant mounted it, and he dug his spurs in its flanks and as fast as the horse could gallop he went. Then the merchant went down to the market-place and he saw me standing in the crowd and he came to me and said, "Why did you make a threatening gesture to my servant when you saw him this morning?"

"That was not a threatening gesture," I said. "It was only a start of surprise. I was astonished to see him in Baghdad, for I had an appointment with him tonight in Samarra."

* * *

My father used to retell this story in his own unique way, but with the same moral. We cannot escape our fate.

Two

A Change of Plans

March 25, 2004 *(journal entry)*
South Seas Hotel
Miami Beach - 6:30 a.m.

*I am sitting under the canopy of the outdoor restaurant in the back of this lovely, newly renovated Art Deco hotel in South Beach on what would have been the third day of our repositioning cruise on the **NCL Crown**. Why am I here, looking out onto the palm trees being whipped around by strong winds while the sun is breaking through for the start of a new day instead of figuring out how to get to the beach in Jamaica where we might find the elderly man with arthritis in his ankles and fingers whose name is Winston and who took us out on his dinghy last month to snorkel along the reef?*

Actually, we arrived at Pier 10 located at the Port of Miami three days ago for our 13-day cruise from Miami to Philadelphia. It was to be an interesting novel way to return home from our Florida vacation. The itinerary was comprised of a day in the Bahamas followed by a day at sea;

then a day in Jamaica and another day at sea; a day in Aruba with one more day at sea before arriving in St. Thomas for a day. After that, the ship would continue northward to Bermuda and then onward to its final destination, the Port of Philadelphia, where the **Crown** would spend the summer months shuttling passengers to and from Bermuda.

Wheeling our bags onto the line designated for Latitudes members, we were handed a rather innocuous-looking sheet of paper by an emotionless man standing at the entrance to the cordoned-off area for "Passengers Only." The message on that sheet of paper changed our plans for the next thirteen days.

Apparently, during the trip from South America to Miami, about three percent of the passengers became ill with the Norwalk virus, a rather debilitating ailment resulting in nausea, vomiting, and headaches. This virus is not uncommon on cruise ships, and with all of the cruises we have taken, we have been fortunate not to have experienced any of the unpleasant symptoms associated with this gastrointestinal bug. Ordinarily, such a warning would not have fazed us, except for the last paragraph of the letter which was signed by the captain of the ship. In it, he stated that should any passenger feel that he would prefer not to go on the cruise because of the outbreak of the Norwalk virus on the previous sailing, then NCL would credit the entire cost of the cruise to a future trip.

This was such an unusual offer that it caused us some concern. Passengers were being detained and were not permitted to board the ship because it was still being sanitized and inspected. We spoke to a representative of NCL, who tried to dissuade us from reneging on our plans and then spoke to the chief purser, who was helpful but ambivalent. The man who checked the passports intimated that he wouldn't go, as did the Miami policeman stationed outside the terminal. So we erred on the side of caution, retrieved our luggage and returned to the South Seas Hotel, where we had just stayed for three days pre-cruise.

Talk of the road not taken! The myriad events that might have taken place are endless. Had we proceeded with our original plans, would

I have won $1000 in the casino or met up with a shark while snorkeling in the Caribbean? Would Steve have become a victim of the Norwalk virus or treated someone medically during one of our excursions, thus saving a life? Or, instead, will I continue to have a nice, restful, and relaxing vacation here in South Beach or will a coconut fall on my head while I am lying lazily on the rope hammock under the palm trees?

Every decision we make, no matter how small or inconsequential, changes the entire course of our lives. It will influence the people we meet, the places we go, the food that we eat, the activities that we engage in, the books that we read, the walks we take - and so on, ad infinitum. The vast number of possibilities boggles the mind.

*I am re-reading Lenny's book, **Things Happen**. His stories, I believe, reflect the indescribable frustration and overwhelming pain that both he and my sister have felt every day since the tragic death of their firstborn son Steven in a car accident twenty years ago. At the time, I felt helpless when they questioned the "what ifs" and the "if onlys." If only he had gone to Columbia University instead of Princeton where he met Doug, the friend with whom he had embarked on his tragically-fated cross-country road trip. If he had opted for Columbia, he wouldn't have met Doug, and he wouldn't have been driving in Arizona where the tragedy occurred. What if he had left a few minutes earlier so that the car would have hit a different tree instead of the one with the low-hanging branch that took his life in an instant? If only he had taken a train. What if I had tried to dissuade him from taking the trip in the first place? The possibilities are endless. But as Lenny says, "Things happen." In fact, according to Jewish law, there are no such things as coincidences. Things happen for a reason and are all part of God's plan.*

As I look out onto the windswept palm trees with the beach beyond, waiting for the sun to break through for the dawn of a new day, I think to myself, "If we were meant to stay at the South Seas Hotel for another nine days, there must be a reason."

Three

There, but for the Grace of God, Go I

"Two roads diverged in a wood, and I—
I took the one less traveled by,
And that has made all the difference."
Robert Frost (1874-1963)

While looking into the genealogy of the Andermans and the Geschwinds, I researched the towns in Europe from which my ancestors emigrated. My father, Simon Anderman, was born in Buczacz in 1910. At that time, Buczacz was part of Austria. In 1918, it was partitioned to Poland, and then, in 1939, it became a part of Ukraine. During the Holocaust, the Nazis tortured and killed and finally decimated the entire Jewish community of Buczacz.

My mother Rosie's family emigrated to America during the first decade of the twentieth century. The Geschwinds came from

Mielec, Poland, where in 1939, on the eve of Rosh Hashanah, the Nazi occupiers of Mielec shot or burned alive the Jews they pulled naked from the *mikvah* (ritual bath). These atrocities persisted, culminating on March 9, 1942, when the Nazi murderers transformed the entire town into a concentration camp.

I marvel at the bravery of my maternal grandparents who came here as teenagers, escaping the anti-Semitism that was pervasive in Mielec, and of my paternal grandmother who, as a thirty-eight-year-old widow with five surviving children, made the onerous trip from Buczacz to America. I cannot help wondering how my family's history would have unfolded had these brave and adventurous souls remained in their respective towns.

I have read two books detailing the horrors that awaited the Jews who lived in the towns that my grandparents so wisely abandoned. *Anatomy of a Genocide: The Life and Death of a Town Called Buczacz* by Omer Bartov, written in 2018, and *Mielec, Poland: The Shtetl That Became a Nazi Concentration Camp* by Rochelle G. Saidel, written in 2012, both bring into focus the harsh reality of what became of the cities that my grandparents had called "home."

Two autobiographies have been written by relatives on both sides of my family who tragically remained in their respective European towns when Hitler came into power. *The Power of Life: Becoming a Human Being* by Pesach Anderman (on my father's side of the family) and *To Vanquish the Dragon* by Pearl Benisch (on my mother's side) are heartbreaking stories that are painfully personal to me. They recount the grueling experiences each suffered as teenagers at the hands of the Nazis during the Holocaust.

Because of their incredible sixth sense of intuition, my grandparents escaped what would have eventually exceeded the horrors of anti-Semitism that they were experiencing in the early part of the twentieth century. Hitler, in his early twenties, had not yet formulated his Final Solution. The brave trailblazers in my family to whom I am forever grateful could not have even imagined the psychopathic levels of inhumanity that Hitler would unleash onto the Jewish people.

So, as the preacher John Bradford is attributed to have said in the early 1500s when he saw a poor criminal being led to his execution, "There, but for the grace of God, go I."

Four

A Change of Profession

"Eeny meeny miny moe. . ."
"The butcher, the baker, the candlestick-maker. . ."
(children's nursery rhymes)

"I'm quitting my job and going to medical school."

I was dumbfounded. I had known my husband since I was six-teen, and never once did he express a desire to go to medical school. Where was this idea coming from?

It was Labor Day weekend, 1967, and my dear mother-in-law was visiting us in Cincinnati, where we had relocated after getting married fifteen months earlier so Steve could pursue his career as a chemical engineer at Procter & Gamble. He had a promising future as the "brand man" for their newly-acquired Folgers Coffee division, having recently developed Folgers Crystals which made the company the leader among its freeze-dried instant coffee competi-tors, Maxwell House's Maxim of General Foods and Nestle's Taster's Choice. So it came as a total and complete surprise to me when he came home that Friday afternoon with his announcement. His mother was flabbergasted! When Steve kept calling me out of the apartment to tell me his intentions, my poor mother-in-law, who loved me like a daughter, was worried that perhaps we were discussing getting a divorce. Actually, it was a kind of divorce, but not from each other. Rather it was Steve from his career. He explained to me that coffee was not good for people to drink, and he did not feel comfortable making the product more tempting for consumers. Although part of his decision was definitely altruistic, I think it had a lot to do with his desire to be his own boss. After almost two years of adjusting to corporate America, where conversations were limited to the weather, baseball, corporate profits, or a favorite restaurant, Steve had become disenfranchised with Procter & Gamble. No one ever talked about religion, politics, or race relations. These topics were strictly verboten. There also seemed to be little appreciation for his hard work and accomplishment in developing Folgers Crystals that ended up saving the company millions of dollars. His only bonus for this breakthrough discovery was the same Butterball turkey that everyone else in the company got for Christmas. He was disillusioned and decided to change gears entirely.

So we went from living in a spanking new two-bedroom apartment with a balcony overlooking a lake in Cincinnati to a two-bedroom, roach-infested, fourteenth-floor apartment in a Mitchell-Lama housing project in New York's East Harlem, conveniently located just four blocks from New York Medical College. Not only was it a dramatic change for Steve to go back to school, it was quite a change for me as well. I had to reinvent myself from being a graduate student to becoming the sole breadwinner. I needed to figure out how to earn a living, and I eventually landed what would become my dream job, teaching in the Speech Department at my alma mater, City College. So while I pursued a career in the academic setting, Steve adjusted to his renewed life as a student. It did not take long for us to become acclimated to our new roles, and we fell into a routine of teaching for me and learning and studying for him. We now faced an uncertain future, unsure of where our new endeavors would take us. We had changed paths at the proverbial fork in the road.

Eight years and three offspring later, Steve became a full-fledged ear, nose, and throat specialist. After working for an established ENT group for one year, he hung up a shingle and opened his own medical office. It was at that juncture in our married life that I gave up my career as a tenured professor and decided to work side by side with Steve for the next thirty years.

Instead of an upward path in corporate America, Steve took the road not taken, starting a new career from the bottom up. Would he have become an executive with a guaranteed pension in a Fortune 500 company? Would I have entertained other top-level executives in my home, living in a fancy house in Cincinnati? Instead, Steve became a busy physician in Northern New Jersey, and I became the office manager/audiologist/administrative assistant in charge of a medical office. I wore many hats in a job that I learned on the fly. When I lament that I left my dream job to work in a medical office, I wonder what might have happened had I stayed at City College, which was located in a dangerous neighborhood in New York City. Crime was not a stranger to Harlem, and the park adjacent to where I walked along St. Nicholas Terrace was rampant with robberies and assaults. Instead, my work environment was in an upscale New Jersey town where walking the streets any time of day or night was never a concern.

Now looking through that rearview mirror, I cannot say with all honesty that we made the best decision. Working together definitely strengthened our relationship. As our children like to say, we are joined at the hip in a way that I do not believe would have happened if we had remained in our two separate careers. Yes, I lost my pension from City College, and certainly Steve, in old age, does not enjoy the handsome benefits he would have had if he stayed at Procter & Gamble. But because we can never go back and have a do-over, I can only say that we made the best decision we could at the time. And for that I am grateful.

Five

A Change of Flight

We had been celebrating our tenth wedding anniversary at Blue-beard's Castle Hotel in St. Thomas. It had just been built, and there were a multitude of glitches that needed to be corrected, so we relocated to the Morningstar Hotel right on the beach where I was totally relaxed and having a great time. But Steve was anxious to return home a week before our scheduled flight. A busy solo physi-cian and surgeon, he did not want to leave his practice unattended for too long while we were vacationing in St. Thomas. I tried to change his mind, but he was adamant. So we changed our flight to one week earlier.

We were seated in the first row of coach, as close to first class as possible. There was a curtain separating the passengers in first class from those of us in coach. I recall how nice the first-class flight attendants were to us, a young married couple, as they showered us with the leftover amenities reserved for their first-class passengers, feeding us filet mignon and special desserts. When we started to dis-embark, they even gave us a whole cake that had not been touched.

A week later, we were shocked to hear that the exact flight we had taken the week before had crashed into the mountains surrounding the Cyril E. King Airport in Charlotte Amalie, St. Thomas. It was the flight that we had originally been scheduled to take. Most likely, the very same crew that had been so kind to us were among those killed in that crash.

"There, but for the grace of God. . . ."

Six

A Pox on Your House

It was to be our dream house - a lovely Tudor built in the 1940s within walking distance to Cedar Lane, Teaneck's main street that boasted a variety of restaurants and boutiques and its own movie theater to boot! The house was conveniently located near Route 4, which would have made Steve's commute to work at his hospital in New York City and my commute to City College a cinch. The neighbors seemed nice, and the teenage boy next door came across as being polite and respectful.

It was 1974. I was a thirty-year-old married woman with two toddlers. I had just gotten tenure at City College in New York, ensuring a steady income, and Steve was finishing up his residency at Einstein Hospital in the Bronx, so we were finally in the financial position to purchase a house. The timing was perfect; the price was perfect; and it was the perfect house for us. Everything had fallen into place. We had signed the contract and were awaiting the attorney review and execution of the contract by the seller.

So you can imagine our disappointment when we were informed

that the seller had backed out of the deal because he had been offered a higher price and decided to proceed with another purchaser. There was no further negotiation, and the spoils went to the higher bidder. The competing buyers were also a young family with a young wife and small children. So we brushed ourselves off and purchased another home that was vastly different from our dream house. We settled for a brand-new split-level, the polar opposite of the charming Tudor we had our hearts set on. It was also $25,000 more expensive, not within walking distance to the main drag, and it lacked all of the nooks and crannies that the older more historic home had to offer.

But everything has a way of working out for the best. It turned out that the nice, polite teenager next door was not so nice after all. Shortly after his new neighbors moved in, he raped the wife of the new homeowner who was eerily similar to me in both age and appearance. It could have easily been me. Once again, I thought, *There but for the grace of God, go I.*

The Road Not Taken

Robert Frost (1874-1963)

Two roads diverged in a yellow wood,
And sorry I could not travel both
And be one traveler, long I stood
And looked down one as far as I could
To where it bent in the undergrowth;

Then took the other, as just as fair,
And having perhaps the better claim,
Because it was grassy and wanted wear;
Though as for that the passing there
Had worn them really about the same,

And both that morning equally lay
In leaves no step had trodden black.
Oh, I kept the first for another day!
Yet knowing how way leads on to way,
I doubted if I should ever come back.

I shall be telling this with a sigh
Somewhere ages and ages hence:
Two roads diverged in a wood, and I -
I took the one less traveled by,
And that has made all the difference.

PART THREE

Roadblocks to Success

One

Dreams That Simmer on the Back Burner

What happens to a dream deferred?
Does it dry up
Like a raisin in the sun?
Or fester like a sore -
And then run?
Does it stink like rotten meat?
Or crust and sugar over -
like syrupy sweet?
Maybe it just sags
like a heavy load.
Or does it explode?

Langston Hughes (1901-1967)

April 6, 1991 *(journal entry)*

Juggling many things at once and trying to keep too many balls in the air at the same time has compromised the quality of my accomplishments to a level that I would describe as merely acceptable - mediocre at best. I have always worked, but no work of art has been signed by me, and no volume of literature bears my name. I have envisioned many goals, but circumstances have prevented me from reaching them. A pioneer in the field of English as a Second Language, I started writing one of the first textbooks on the subject. That was back in the late 1960s, long before ESL was a well-known entity. The book never materialized. Another idea for a book called **The Making of a Doctor's Wife** never got off the ground, and the magazine articles about topics ranging from water shortages to phonetic mispronunciations among my ESL students or the deleterious effects of eating black licorice are yet unpublished.

At the expense of not having my initials etched in the corner of a beautiful painting or my name listed in the **New York Times Book Review,** I have developed strong and deep family relationships. I have worked hard to help build my husband's career, which is so enmeshed with my own life that I do not think I could separate our two lives and careers even if I tried. His profession is part of my identity. "We" went to medical school, even though I was not the one who had to take the grueling exams, and I do not have the distinction of having an "M.D." after my name. Working together to reach common goals has increased my self-esteem and has created a strong bond that could never have been achieved had I done my own thing.

I have placed some of my own aspirations on the back burner. Like many mothers, I have been chauffeur, shopper, worker, mediator, referee, counselor, and teacher. I have tried to smooth the road for my children, shielding them as best I could from the bumps and hurdles they will inevitably encounter despite my best efforts to protect them.

January 3, 2001 - *(journal entry)*

I was thinking the other day that our lives are defined by our actions. Even though the concept is not terribly unique or profound, I realize that my life has been (and still is) defined by the things I **must** do. I seem to gain both my greatest fulfillment and biggest frustration by completing tasks that must get done, while neglecting the things I would prefer doing. This dichotomy of two diametrically opposite feelings, fulfillment vs frustration, has been a persistent cause of angst for me. Out of necessity, I have become accustomed to completing those obligations which I have no choice but to meet and then hoping to dive into what I would really rather be doing. But when I finish the former, I am usually too tired or busy with some other "necessary" chore to do the latter. It is like the old adage to eat your vegetables first and **then** enjoy dessert, only to find that you are too full to even attempt one bite! I once saw the very same message displayed on a T-shirt: "Life is short. Eat dessert first!"

I suppose it is a habit I developed in order to survive. Paying the bills, completing work for the office, answering phone calls, filling out forms, writing letters, handling problems with patients, meeting deadlines, and arguing with insurance companies, all the while carting children to school, doctors' appointments, dance classes, Cub Scouts and Brownies (not to mention shopping and cooking) all took precedence over my own personal goals that were always put at the bottom of the pile or on the back burner. My closet is filled with boxes of photographs from thirty years ago still in disarray. I have bins of unfinished baby blankets started when my grown children were infants. My journals have spotty entries with missing months and even years.

Seventeen years ago, I had an eye-opening conversation with my father's oncologist. He told me that because most of his patients have less than a year to live, he restructures his priorities every day. What we think is so very important really isn't that urgent in the greater scheme of things. But changing our priorities is not an easy task. How do I put the spinach and broccoli at the bottom of the pile and put the luscious fruits and fine chocolates on the top? I have come to realize that it is important for me to change gears altogether so that what had been pushed aside as being secondary will now surface to the top stamped "**HIGH PRIORITY.**"

So, this morning, instead of doing the laundry, running to the post office, bringing in the snowblower for repair, calling PSE&G about my mother's inflated utility bill, calling the lab to correct the insurance information for Steve's blood test, carrying the bottles out for recycling, faxing information to an insurance company, and a few other mundane chores, I told myself that I should have first and foremost prioritized putting photos into albums, practiced singing along with my **Les Miserables** CD album, finished the baby blanket I started for Emily twenty-seven years ago, written in the "Grandmother's Journal" that Avis gave me three-and-a-half years ago when Sarah, my first grandchild, was born, poured out my thoughts in this book of memoirs, sat by the fireplace, and relished in life and its phenomenal beauty. But sadly, I did none of those things.

We are creatures of habit, and all we can do is try to make a serious, conscious effort to back-pedal and prioritize what is really important to us and to devote our lives to what we find fulfilling and satisfying.

* * *

January 5, 2001 *(two days later)* **journal entry**

I heard the garbage truck pick up other people's bottles and cans for recycling while I was busy writing in my journal. I left the breakfast dishes in the sink and didn't rush to the post office to mail some letters. And guess what? Nothing bad happened!

Two

Reflections on the Violin

Perched on top of my bookcase sits the half-size violin I played as a young child. One might ask why I have it displayed so prominently.

In 1966, I read a short story about a young man who always wanted to be a violinist. He practiced every day so that he could accomplish his goal. But as he got older, he became so involved in educating himself, finding a job, getting married, supporting his family, and doing the things he felt he had to do in order to survive that he gave up playing the violin and placed it on the top shelf of his closet, promising himself that one day, when he was not so busy, he would rekindle his dream. But he never did; and at the end of the story, the man, now old and feeble, opens the door to the closet and looks up. He stares at the violin with tears in his eyes, realizing that he has waited too long to accomplish his dream.

Reading the short story as a twenty-two-year-old newly married graduate student, I vowed right then and there that I would never suffer the same fate as that disappointed violinist. The words of the poet Robert Burns ring true. In 1786, he wrote, "The best laid plans of mice and men often go awry;" and now, fifty years after first reading that story, I saw the proverbial violin sitting atop my bookcase, a stark reminder of my own dreams deferred.

Three

On Self-Confidence (Or Lack Thereof!)

"Cherish the failures for they are part of the journey forward."
Torah - *Parsha Vayelech*

July 10, 2003 - Midnight *(journal entry)*

I cannot sleep. I keep thinking about why it is that I lacked the confidence since childhood to make a genuine effort to realize my dreams. As a first-grader, I wished I could draw a picture of a dog as beautifully as Carola Dibbell. When we moved to Spring Valley and I entered Mr. Miller's fifth-grade class for the first time, I tried to hide my nervousness behind my flowing brown hair tied neatly in back with the big white bow that my sister Pearl made for me the night before. I didn't believe I was as creative as my classmates when they wrote a play about early America, and their characters whom they called "Ma" and "Pa" seemed so much more inventive than I could ever imagine. Good grades and glowing comments by my teachers did little to boost my self-esteem; and even winning the coveted American Legion oratorical contest in my senior year hardly changed my belief that I could never really succeed.

I was a self-defeatist. Always a good writer and loving it, I thought of writing a book, but I would go to the library, surrounded by thousands of volumes, and ask myself what one more book would add to the plethora of literature already in print. Did Emily Dickinson ask herself why the world needed more love poetry? Did Stephen King believe that horror stories had all been told? Did Agatha Christie wonder if Inspector Poirot had solved every mystery? Or did Charles Dickens question why it was so important to write about the London of his time? How about Bernard Malamud, whom I had the privilege of hearing speak at our common alma mater, City College. He confessed that he had a "C" average in English (mine was an "A"), and yet he had the perseverance, self-confidence, drive, and fortitude to become one of the best American authors of the 20th century.

Why is it that I never completed the pursuit to write what might very well have been the first textbook on ESL (English as a Second Language) when few educators and even fewer laymen knew what ESL even stood for? In 1969, I was a pioneer in developing the first ESL program at my university, so it was the perfect time to convert my original class notes into a textbook. I wish I had an answer.

But as I approach my third score, I finally have the courage to bare my heart as openly as I have in my manuscript, **Rosie (and me)**. Writing is like taking an x-ray of one's soul. It exposes the inner self for all to see, to examine, to analyze and to evaluate. It takes courage. The author, Dani Shapiro, aptly calls writer's block, "a failure of nerve."

July 3, 2011
Starbucks ~ 8:15 a.m. *(journal entry)*

Time slips by. Days become weeks; weeks become months; and months morph into years. How casually we treat each day as though our days were limitless. I realize how cavalier I am about my days, procrastinating over, for example, finishing my **Rosie** *manuscript. It is only during quiet times like now, sipping my latte and reflecting on my life that I truly realize just how limited my time really is. I am then incentivized to trudge on with those things that are very important to me but to which I merely give lip service. I get inspired for the moment; but then, for whatever reason, the enthusiasm wanes and I am once again stuck in a state of inertia, acting as if I have all the time in the world. At sixty-seven, clearly this is not the case. So I am determined to rally and finally finish my decades-long project and at least move the scribblings of* **Rosie** *off the yellow pad and enter them into the computer.*

* * *

January 12, 2013 *(journal entry)*

I'm trying to figure out why I am having such trouble completing my manuscript. In an effort to make my surroundings more conducive to writing, I have rearranged my guest room with the desk in front of the window, a comfortable rocking chair, and rose-scented candles. My goal is to publish my memoir this year because it will be Rosie's 100th birthday!

* * *

Several years ago, when **Rosie (and me)** was in its infancy stages of development, a passing dream really, I registered for a seminar through a group called Media Bistro appropriately called "Memoir

Writing." It sounded perfect for me. I still have the special note-book I bought for the momentous occasion.

I drove into New York City filled with hope and anticipation. It was held in the instructor's opulent apartment on the Upper East Side of Manhattan. Her living room was filled to capacity with aspiring memoir writers, each of whom was to present a three-minute reading of their manuscript. After I read a small portion of the unbreakable bond between Rosie and me, the forty-something instructor, impressed with herself and probably gloating at how she managed to get dozens of suckers to shell out $150 each for her class, interrupted my presentation, pummeling me with a barrage of questions: *What was so extraordinary about your mother? Was she in the Holocaust? Did she invent anything? Did she write a book or paint a famous painting? Did she do anything that made her special?* I was mortified.

Easily discouraged, I put **Rosie** aside, filled with the desire to publish a book but lacking the determination and courage to do so. The experience in New York was all I needed to retreat back into my self-defeatist attitude and give up any hope of ever completing my lifelong goal.

But then I began thinking. Rosie may not have accomplished any of the things that would make her famous, but, in fact, she was very special, and her story deserved to be told. She was what some might call "ordinary," but, in actuality, she was a most extraordinary woman, and I felt compelled to write her story.

Unfortunately, because of self-doubt and procrastination, it would take another twenty years for the publication of Rosie's story to become a reality.

* * *

It is a self-fulfilling prophesy. When we say we cannot do some-thing, we can't and we don't. It becomes a vicious cycle. If only I had developed a more positive self-concept earlier in my life. I am reminded of a professor I had in graduate school who said, "Nothing breeds success like success; and nothing breeds failure like failure." So many of my journal entries over the past three decades allude to my desire to achieve my writing goals, but nothing ever got done. Just remember, it is never too late. Listen to your heart and don't get discouraged by what others say. Have confidence in yourself. Keep in mind the motivational words of Nelson Mandela: "It always seems impossible until it's done."

Ironically, it was my mother who used to tell me, "You're as good, if not better, than the next person!" I wish now that I had taken her advice to heart long ago, but unfortunately, I did not. Despite many accomplishments, I never really felt convinced that I was that good. Looking back, I cannot fathom why I was not encouraged when Professor Sherwin, my college English professor, a renowned historian and published author, gave me an A-plus on my short story and wrote "Expert Writing!" on the top of the page. Why didn't I run with it and pursue my dream of writing? Why was it that I allowed my self-doubt and sense of defeatism to dominate? I was twenty years old. But as my mother Rosie used to say, "You can't put an old head on young shoulders."

Now that I am in the throes of my seventh decade of life, I realize how foolish I was not to have had more self-confidence for so many years. How wasteful I was of the time I had; how many years I allowed to lapse when I could have been more productive. Now I feel as though I have to get in my "last licks" to accomplish what I should have been doing all these years. But, as they say, "Better late than never." So I am taking the bull by the horns and moving full speed ahead to complete this second book, *Vignettes on Life*. After all: "Life is like a roll of toilet paper. The closer you get to the end, the faster it goes!"

Four

On Writing and Procrastination

December 1, 2019 *(journal entry)*

(Author's note: I just opened this document I entitled "ON WRITING" and guess what! The page is blank! So I changed it to "ON WRITING AND PROCRASTINATION")

* * *

"Sometimes I have thought it would be an excellent rule to live each day as if we should die tomorrow. Such an attitude would emphasize sharply the values of life. We should live each day with a gentleness, a vigor, and a keenness of appreciation which are often lost when time stretches before us in the constant panorama of more days and months and years to come."

Helen Keller, *Three Days to See*

*Procrastination rears its ugly head throughout all of my journal entries, where I repeatedly alluded to finishing my memoir about my mother until it was finally published in 2017. Today's journal entry demonstrates the dichotomy of my constant battle between being productive and falling into the abyss of procrastination. Imagine! I have even been procrastinating about finishing a chapter called "On Procrastination" for my new book, **Vignettes on Life***!*

* * *

March 4, 2020 **(journal entry)**
7:10 a.m.
Cherry Hill, NJ

*Every morning for the past few weeks, I have been waking up determined to work on a chapter I call "On Procrastination" for my new book **Vignettes on Life,** and every morning, I find something else to do instead. For instance, this morning, even though I am trying to focus on writing that chapter, my mind is cluttered thinking about other things I should be doing. "I'll clean the balcony floor (should I use a mop or the new scrubbing machine I bought?)" or "I'll pay my Amazon bill by phone" or "I'll start putting away my winter clothes now that the weather has turned mild" or...or...or...!*

*With the brutal realization that I am closer to eighty than seventy, I have decided to finish that chapter by tomorrow. I will start immediately! Well, that is, **after** I have my coffee and clean out the dishwasher!*

Flashbacks. . . .

August 23, 2003 *(journal entry)*

    *The summer is drawing to a close, and I am entering the autumn of my life. I realize that time is limited, and I know I do not have the luxury of allowing weeks, months, even years to elapse between writing my memoirs. I began writing **My Turn** more than a decade ago. I can remember vividly sitting down at my then new CAT computer/word processor in my small guest room in Allendale, New Jersey, typing away incessantly for hours. Uninterrupted, I completed eight pages in just a few hours, thinking "I will finish this in no time." But, alas, it was the same old story, and all I have now to show for that effort are those same eight pages.*

* * *

January 30, 2004 *(journal entry)*
Bergenfield, NJ

    On the eve of the third anniversary of my mother's death, I bought $50 worth of yarn and knitted a scarf. Then I went back to the yarn store and bought another $40 worth. I'm scratching my head trying to figure out the symbolism here.

    About eight months ago, I completed a draft of a book of memoirs primarily about my mother. I wanted to tweak the details, add some more imagery and bring the book to a level where I felt comfortable showing it to an agent or a publisher. But I haven't done that yet. Knitting is an excellent source of solace and procrastination. So I am knitting scarves instead of completing my literary project. Hopefully, I will get to the book before the last scarf is finished!

May 14, 2004 *(journal entry)*
Bergenfield, NJ

Another Mother's Day has come and gone, and the manuscript called **Rosie** *remains untouched since I stopped working on it almost a year ago. I have fantasized that the book honoring my mother would be released on Mother's Day, but clearly this has not happened. I shall view this time, not as five days too late, but 360 days early for the next Mother's Day deadline. How I would love to share my thoughts and experiences, along with my mother's bravery and optimism with others. But at the same time, I suppose I am fearful of the outcome. I do not want to diminish in any way the positive relationship I enjoyed with my mother by having critics and editors tear it apart and judge its worth. So I am torn between whether to proceed with trying to publish my memoirs or to be content having them at my fingertips for my own gratification. One way or another, I hope to make a decision prior to next Mother's Day.*

* * *

September 10, 2009 *(journal entry)*
Grindhouse Cafe
Haddonfield, NJ 10:40 a.m.

Rosie *has been an albatross around my neck waiting to be freed since my mother's death in 2001. The manuscript has followed me from Allendale to Bergenfield, traveled around the country with us on our road trip from 2006 to 2007, and now, like the violin, it is comfortably sitting in full view in my apartment in Haddonfield. Today, for the first time in three years, I have taken my rough draft out of the file cabinet and placed it on my white wicker desk in the living/dining room. My heart wants to work on it and have it published, but I haven't been able to bring myself* around to doing anything with it. I am reminded of an essay my son, Todd, wrote for one of his college applications. In it, he talks about a monster lurking in the corner of the room. That monster turns out to be the pile of college applications waiting to be filled out! I have the same inertia and paralysis in completing my own project. Maybe it is because I am not sure what to do next.

* * *

Rosh Hashanah 5770 (Jewish New Year) *(journal entry)*
September 21, 2009
Grindhouse Cafe - 10:01 a.m.

Rosh Hashanah. A time to reflect and look forward to the new year. A time to make amends and decide what to do differently in the coming year.

At the age of sixty-five (can that be?), I realize that procrastination is no longer a luxury I can afford, and so I have decided, yet again, to pursue the goals that I have let slide over the past few years. It is no secret that my journal entries have consistently addressed the issue of publishing a memoir about my mother Rosie. Despite my cries of determination over the years, procrastination always managed to prevail. Last night, I dreamt that I was telling someone about my mother and how I had written a book about her. I had been talking about it for so long that the person in my dream was surprised that it had not yet been published. So this morning, I decided to set up a schedule for myself and finally get the show on the road!

February 21, 2010 *(journal entry)*
Grindhouse Cafe
Haddonfield, NJ

It is Sunday at the Grindhouse Cafe, crowded with people working on their computers, reading the Sunday newspaper, even playing a game of **Scrabble**. I am listening to the broken record that keeps playing in my head that has consumed me for so many years: "Why is **Rosie** still not finished?" My writing has become more sparse, less frequent. Not only have I not been prolific, but my thoughts are less profound, and I feel as though I have succeeded in reaching an unsatisfying state of mediocrity. I constantly think of getting back to my manuscript, but so far...nothing. I don't know why I am so paralyzed when it comes to doing something with it - publish, revise, embellish. Perhaps I do not have the will to achieve closure, or maybe it is fear of failure or rejection. But Rosie's is a story I feel compelled to share. Next year will be ten years since she died, and **Rosie** has yet to reach the masses.

I know how long it has been because Aviva Raisl, Rosie's first namesake born just five weeks after her passing, is nine, going on ten years old. When she saw the manuscript on the desk, she asked, "Grandma. Is this a book?" When I told her it was, she exclaimed, "You should publish it. Then you will make a lot of money."

Actually, I would like to publish it for many reasons, the least of which is to make a lot of money. First and foremost, I would like to publish it to honor my mother and to get her story out there. Secondly, I would like to publish it to have the satisfaction of completing something I started so long ago. What am I waiting for?

November 10, 2010 *(journal entry)*
Starbucks
Cherry Hill, NJ

*I was wondering today during my walk here to Starbucks why I have been so hesitant about finally getting **Rosie** published. In the past, I completed important things without delay. Reviews to insurance companies, filling out medical forms, meeting important obligations for the office, the children, and the house all got done promptly. Perhaps, I am worried that it will be the final achievement of my life, and once this goal has been achieved, well, what is left? Will my purpose here on earth be done? I hope that the completion of **Rosie (and me)** won't be my swan song, my last hurrah.*

* * *

fast forward. . . . May 5, 2017 *(journal entry)*

*Hallelujah! **Rosie** is published!*

PART FOUR

Becoming

One

The Making of a
Doctor's Wife

The first meeting of the New York Medical College Student Wives Club commenced promptly at 7:30 p.m. on September 4, 1968. About forty young women showed up for that first meeting. Some of them were the wives of upper classmen, but most were the frightened spouses of freshmen who seemed to be searching for comfort and reassurance from others in the same boat. Safety in numbers, I suppose. We had all come to hear a panel of doctors' wives talk about what it was like to be a doctor's wife!

"Just remember," an elderly woman admonished, "from now on, your husband will be married to his profession."

Five years later, when Steve was a surgical intern, he attached his wedding ring to his scrub suit with a safety pin. After the surgery, he threw his soiled scrubs down the laundry chute, forgetting that his wedding ring was still pinned to it. When he realized his mistake, he riffled through all of the dirty laundry to locate the ring, but it was gone forever. The symbolism of losing his wedding ring "to his profession" was not lost on me and seemed to confirm the warning from the woman at the Wives Club meeting so many years earlier.

What was I doing at this meeting with other wives of medical students? Just one year earlier, I was living in a beautiful apartment, drove a brand-new car, and was looking forward to a bright future living in Cincinnati, Ohio. My, how my life had changed!

The start of Steve's pre-medical school career could not have been more discouraging. In an effort to figure out the likelihood of his getting into medical school, Steve met with the pre-med advisor at the University of Cincinnati.

"What are my chances of getting into medical school?" Steve asked hopefully.

"Well," replied the advisor. "Ordinarily, I tell older applicants like yourself not to bother. But in your case, I can't say that."

The advisor clearly recognized Steve's fortitude, determination, and intelligence while he reviewed his impressive resume. Among other things, he was listed in **Who's Who Among College Students**, was president of more than one engineering society, had a perfect score on the math section of the medical school entrance exam, and had graduated third in his class of chemical engineers from a prestigious university.

"So, again," Steve asked. "What are my chances?"

Looking directly into Steve's eyes, the advisor answered, "All I can say is this: Apply and pray!"

At that time, I was a graduate student at the University of Cincinnati, completing my master's degree. There was a young woman in one of my classes who was married to a resident physician. I can remember how much I envied her when she said that her husband was a resident. I loved the way the word resident *(rez-i-dent)* flowed so trippingly on the tongue and hoped that one day I would be able to use that word to describe my own husband. When I told another classmate who was a PhD candidate in psychology about Steve's plans, she cited a study that found the divorce rate among medical students higher than among Hollywood movie stars!

* * *

twenty-six years later . . .
April 11, 1993 *(journal entry)*

Over the course of the past twenty years as a doctor's wife, I have become accustomed to hearing criticism against doctors, but a recent comment by a morning radio talk show host piqued my ire more than ever before. He was discussing President Bill Clinton's new administration's proposed healthcare reform, gloating over the fact that with managed care, doctors would have to "trade in their Mercedes for Mercurys." Doctors have become the convenient scapegoats for the current recession, and even though the public relies on doctors to treat their physical ailments, they have come to blame doctors for their financial ills. Of course, one may argue, coming from a doctor's wife, this writer is naturally biased. Most people believe that doctors just are, always were, never became! A lot has to happen between deciding to go to medical school and finally hanging out a shingle. My purpose here is not to complain about how doctors are being vilified, but rather it is my intention to enlighten the reader about where the doctor came from. How did he get to this point in his career?

I have not always been a doctor's wife. I was married to a chemical engineer for two years, a medical student for four years, an intern for one year, a surgical intern for one year, a specialist resident for four years, and a practicing surgeon and physician for the next fifteen. You see, I have been married to the same man for over twenty-six years! When the average patient visits the doctor, the only thing he or she sees is a successful person who may or may not drive a Mercedes, who receives a lot of money for a short period of time, and who displays some fancy-looking degrees and licenses on the wall. But let me, in this short amount of time and space, try to describe what that physician went through before arriving to where he is now.

On a beautiful June day in 1966, I married my high school sweetheart at the Park Terrace catering hall across the street from Yankee Stadium in the Bronx, New York. I had known Steve for six years, having met when I was sixteen and he was seventeen years old. After we both graduated from City College, he as a chemical engineer and I as a speech major, we got married and moved to Cincinnati, where we embarked on our new life as a married couple with our newly acquired college degrees in tow.

Fifteen months later, on the Friday before Labor Day weekend in the year 1967, my husband came home from work and announced that he wanted to quit his job and go to medical school. I had just finished reading that short story about the man with the long-forgotten violin, and determined not to interfere with Steve's decision, I encouraged him to follow his heart.

The only prerequisite course for medical school that Steve needed was a one-year course in biology. We found out that the nearest university that offered the required course at a time that coincided with our work schedules was at Wright State University in Dayton, some fifty miles away from where we lived in Cincinnati. Two nights a week for the next two semesters, I prepared sandwiches that were to be our dinner, picked Steve up at Procter & Gamble, and drove the fifty miles to Wright State, going the legal speed limit of eighty-five miles per hour.

Once he made up his mind to actually apply to medical school, he contacted the Dean of the Pre-med Department at our alma mater, City College in New York City, who suggested that he apply to a limited number of medical schools (either he would get in or not) and that he would personally contact Steve's engineering professors to obtain letters of recommendation. How clearly I remember sitting on the newly-installed blue wall-to-wall carpet in the middle of our living room, typing out applications on the Smith Corona electric typewriter that my parents had just given me as a college graduation gift. We sent out five applications and said a little prayer.

Applying to medical school was the easy part. Informing his bosses at Procter & Gamble that he was planning to leave their company was another story. It is a known fact that at Procter & Gamble, like other large corporations, if you plan to leave their employ for any reason, you are marched to your desk, asked to clean it out under the auspices of a representative of the company, told to turn in your key and security identification card, escorted to the door, and bid farewell. But they were stymied because Steve had invented a product that was to eventually outsell all of its competitors, and his superiors were not anxious to see him go. So when Steve told them that he was planning to go to medical school, rather than firing him on the spot, they convened behind closed doors for the entire day. It was not only his immediate bosses, but it was their bosses as well, and even higher higher-ups. Finally, at 5:30 that afternoon, those in charge at Winton Hill's research center for the development of Folgers Coffee filed out of the room and met with my husband. They told him that after careful consideration, they had come to the unprecedented decision to allow him to continue working even though they realized that he would be leaving at the end of June. They even offered to reduce his workload so that he could have more time to study for his course at Wright State.

*But the hardest step was yet to come. I had to tell my father! My father was old school, and especially in the mid-1960s before women had fully joined the workforce, he felt that when a man got married, his obligation was to his wife and future family. I knew how my father might react, so instead of telling him over the phone, I wrote him a letter. I explained to him that his new son-in-law was thinking, **just thinking**, that perhaps he might decide one day to go to dental school or maybe even* *medical school (this was after the applications were already in the admissions offices of five medical colleges!). I was not there when my father read the letter, but I learned from my sister-in-law that all of my fears and predictions about his reaction were accurate. He was not angry, but, as I had anticipated, he felt that it was irresponsible. (Ironically, almost two decades later, it was Steve's medical expertise and Herculean efforts that prolonged my father's life an extra year when he was terminally ill with acute leukemia.)*

With all of my clearheadedness about sending away for applications and helping to fill them out, I began to feel tremendous anxiety. I suddenly realized that I would become the sole breadwinner; I would have to be alone while my husband was studying long into the night and on weekends; I would be stuck in a five-year situation of financial struggle and uncertainty about the future. In order to avoid feeling overwhelmed, I decided to view the medical school period of time not as a five-year block but rather to take it one day at a time. Life would go on. We were not going to be living in a vacuum. There would be work, family, shopping, watching television, and babies - just like other couples who were not in medical school.

We moved back to New York, where Steve attended New York Medical College, completed his internship and residencies (I finally got to use that lovely word, rez-i-dent), and took a position with a group of established ear, nose, and throat physicians. After one year, he decided to hang up his own shingle and opened a solo practice. It was then that I relinquished my tenure at City College, a position I loved, and began to work in his office full-time as his office manager and audiologist.

I can remember clearly the night before we opened the doors of our new medical practice. It was three o'clock in the morning, and I was scrubbing the tile floor of the bathroom, bent like a pretzel, unable to stand up. I looked up and said to Steve, "It's great being a doctor's wife!"

Steve became one of the busiest specialists in our area until managed care came along and completely decimated his practice. So in

2006, unable to afford to keep our doors open, we retired, or as I like to tell people, "Managed care retired us."

We sold our house and spent almost a year traveling around the country, the road trip being one of the most interesting and rewarding experiences of our lives. We saw our children get married; we buried our parents; we rejoiced in the births of thirteen grandchildren; I wrote and published a memoir, **Rosie (and me)**; and now we are retired, living carefully within our means in a beautiful condo in Cherry Hill, New Jersey.

So that, my dear readers, is the rise and fall of a medical career. It is the making of a doctor's wife in a nutshell!

THE MARRIAGE PROPOSAL

(Note: This entry was not included in my original manuscript, but the story is so intriguing to my grandchildren that I decided to add it so that my progeny will know the real story of the marriage proposal!)

After we moved to Spring Valley in 1955, I worked summers at my aunt's hotel as a mother's helper. Young mothers stayed at the hotel all summer while their husbands worked in New York City during the week and joined their wives on the weekends. It was at the hotel that I learned how to dance the cha-cha, Lindy Hop, and fox trot from the gay dance instructor, Jerry Stout, one of the few gay men who had come out of the closet in the 1950s and who my aunt called a fairy. "Gay" was not a term yet to be used by the homosexual community. It wouldn't appear for decades to come. As the years went by, I switched from being a mother's helper to working behind the front desk at the hotel. It was there during the Jewish High Holidays of 1960 that a young busboy asked for more blankets for the bunk he was sleeping on in the staff quarters. It turned out that he was the busboy for the table that my family and I ate at in the dining room. Steve was seventeen, cute, hardworking; and I caught his attention by spilling Chinese food on him in the kitchen (deliberately, I suppose; **definitely**, according to Steve). We spent as much time together for the entire week and were caught off-guard when my father saw us stealing a kiss by the Coke machine on the outside patio.

Over the next year, we saw each other intermittently (my father felt that once a month was enough for his sixteen-year-old youngest daughter to date the same person); and Steve made the three-hour sojourn by bus from the Bronx to Spring Valley. It was true love! Sometimes we met in Fort Lee, where my newly-married sister Pearl lived with her husband Lenny. But never having dated much before, I wasn't sure I wanted an exclusive relationship, even though I loved Steve dearly and could never imagine myself ending up with anyone else. Admittedly, I gave Steve a tough time, and finally, in our junior year at City College in New York, where we both went to school, he decided he had enough of my on-again, off-again relationship, and we broke up.

In the fall of 1965, I bumped into him in Shepard Hall on the North Campus of CCNY. We hadn't seen or spoken to each other in several months, and he told me that after he graduated in January, he was starting a job at Proctor & Gamble in Cincinnati. As we were crossing Amsterdam Avenue to have lunch at the kosher deli, I declared, "Then I guess we should get married." It might have been dangerous to make such a statement in the middle of traffic, but he said "yes" and we celebrated over our turkey and pastrami sandwiches. Two months later, we were engaged and got married six months after that.

Two

From Dream to Reality

"It always seems impossible until it's done."
Nelson Mandela

Rosie (and me) was published in 2017, just nine days before Mother's Day and a month shy of my seventy-third birthday. I am reminded of the biblical matriarch, Sarah, who laughs when she tells God, "Imagine Sarah - having a baby at the age of ninety." I feel the same way. "Imagine Carol - publishing a memoir at the age of seventy-two!"

* * *

Many people have asked me how I came to write a book about my mother. I have been keeping journals since 1988. The consistent theme throughout my seven personal journals has been the inner conflict between my aspiration to write a memoir and my continuous frustration at not completing that goal. Even though I was consumed with the desire to tell the story of the unbreakable bond between my mother and myself combined with her relentless courage in dealing with her own physical hardships, I found myself in a constant state of inertia. It was an ongoing mantra: *What's holding me back?* or *Why can't I finish this?*

People handle grief in different ways. I dealt with the grief of my mother's death in 2001 through writing, a process that I found to be extremely cathartic during that very sad period of my life. After her death, I spent a week writing about her continuously, morning, noon, and night. The words incessantly poured out from my heart. I was merely a conduit, channeling the jumble of memories in my head bursting to be told into a journal filled with blank pages. Looking over those journal entries, I came to realize that Rosie's compelling story had to be told.

Over the next few years, I made half-hearted attempts to write a book about my mother. A common thread throughout many of my journal entries was my lament at not having achieved my goal but with the underlying hope to finish the book by Mother's Day, so appropriate because of the dynamics of the mother-daughter relationship in **Rosie (and me)**. But, year after year, Mother's Days came and went with no book to mark the day.

I insinuated myself into situations where I tried to identify myself as a writer. I attended a lecture on memoir writing at the local library. The speaker told us that most people became discouraged because it might take a year or more to write a book. "Just remember," she smiled, "the year will pass by anyway - whether you write the book or not - so you may just as well write the book!"

Then I took a one-day seminar on publishing. The instructor assured me that memoirs were popular because people like to eavesdrop on other people's lives. I even joined the Writers Roundtable at the Cherry Hill Library. After all, I concluded, if I attended the "writers" roundtable, wasn't I then, by definition, a "writer?"

At the age of seventy-two, I enrolled in a writer's symposium at

Hunter College in New York City. Meeting with other novice writers like myself, as well as publishers and published authors, made me aware that I was not alone in my concerns as a first-time author. There were others who were just as uncertain and confused as I.

Although these experiences were encouraging and put me in a better frame of mind about my writing, they did not diminish the negativity I still felt gnawing at me from the blow to my ego I received at that first seminar in memoir writing at the arrogant teacher's apartment on the Upper East Side of Manhattan. Her questioning the validity of writing about my mother, who, to an outsider, appeared to be just an ordinary person, sucked every ounce of self-confidence out of me, forcing me into a state of inertia.

* * *

Those who have succeeded in achieving an important goal can usually look back and identify clear turning points in their lives that shaped the realization of that dream. For me, there were two major events that led to the publication of *Rosie (and me)*.

The main turning point occurred the summer before the book was published when I serendipitously stopped at a table at a local fair where a young woman named Stefani Milan was selling her recently self-published book. I told her how smart she was to have followed her dream while she was still a young woman and not wait until she was in her seventies, like me, frustrated at never having published a book. I expected her to look at me sympathetically but unfazed by my dilemma. Instead, the response from this virtual stranger was, "Well, why don't you? I'll tell you how I did it." Her encouragement boosted my enthusiasm and renewed the optimism I once had, and I found myself believing that finishing and publishing my memoir was truly possible. After many revisions and meetings with Stefani (who I call my guardian angel), I finally completed a draft of *Rosie (and me)*. None of the five literary agents I approached were interested in representing a seventy-two-year-old first-time author, so it became clear that self-publishing was the way to go. With the patience of a saint, Stefani deftly led me through the complicated maze of self-publishing.

There was another unexpected and certainly unwanted turning point for me, not only for publishing my book, but for my life in general. At the end of the summer of 2016, my sister-in-law Susan was diagnosed with advanced liver cancer that had metastasized from her pancreas. Susan had so much to live for - a wonderful marriage, great kids, loving grandchildren, money, and homes. She always felt she had longevity on her side because she led a healthy lifestyle and her mother had lived to a hundred and three. So when she was especially tired and went for a blood test, she could not possibly have expected such a grave diagnosis. On January 4th, 2017, I found myself on a plane heading from Philadelphia to San Francisco to say my final good-bye to Susan. My heart broke when I saw the once vibrant happy woman I had known for almost six decades, lying motionless in bed, sleeping mostly, a shadow of the woman she once was. When I came into her room, her eyes opened wide and she smiled, telling me how happy she was to see me. Three days later, she was gone.

Susan's illness and eventual death reinforced my firm belief that one's life can turn on a dime, and I said to myself, "Carol, what the hell are you waiting for?" I had known Susan ever since she met my brother when she was sixteen. As far back as I can remember, Susan always insisted, "This is not a dress rehearsal. Do what you want to do NOW!" And she certainly practiced what she preached.

I took her advice to heart and finally accomplished what I had been talking about for decades. *Rosie (and me)* has been published!

Three

What I Learned from an
Immigrant

This is the story of two first-generation immigrants. Both were writers, but only one of them cultivated and further pursued his natural abilities. The other was my father.

In 1913, at the age of three, my father, Simon Anderman, came to the United States from Austria. His thirty-eight-year-old widowed mother left the only life she had ever known to come to America in order to spare her children from the horrific conditions that Jews had endured for centuries in Buczacz (a town that was part of Austria, then taken over by Poland in 1918, and annexed by Ukraine in 1939).

But life in America was far from perfect. Simon and his family lived in a tenement on the Lower East Side of New York City, where the "toilet was in the yard" and his mother took in boarders to help pay the rent. Bullied by his classmates, he often asked if he could leave school early, lying to his teacher that he had a doctor's

96

appointment in order to avoid being chased all the way home by predominantly Irish Catholic hooligans whose goal was to beat up the skinny Jewish Christ-killer, who was my father. But despite this, my father loved America and all that it stood for.

Unable to attend college when he was a young man, my father enrolled in the local community college when he was fifty-three. As a twenty-year-old college student, I recognized the writing skills that my father possessed while I typed the handwritten stories he penned for his freshman English composition class. I often wonder how different his life might have been had he been fortunate enough to have had the opportunity to pursue his natural writing talent. What would it have been like for him if he wasn't the youngest child of a widow from Eastern Europe who worked in a sweatshop, forcing her either to leave her three-year-old toddler home alone or to lie about his age so he could enroll in kindergarten? What might his life have been like if he had been born into a family where his writing talents were recognized and nurtured?

Might he have become a famous writer, smoked a pipe, and dressed in tweed jackets with suede patches at the elbows? Perhaps he would have hobnobbed with other writers of his day like F. Scott Fitzgerald, J.D. Salinger, Upton Sinclair, and the notorious Dorothy Parker at the famous "Round Table" in the Pergola Room on the third floor of the Algonquin Hotel in New York City. Is it not possible that his name might have been as well known as S.Y. Agnon, another immigrant born in Buczacz, who became a Nobel Prize laureate and is recognized as one of Israel's most notable authors? Could he have avoided becoming a delivery boy in a cleaning store that he eventually owned, thus defying his ultimate fate of dying of acute leukemia some thirty years after giving up the dry cleaning store where he slaved in the unbearable heat of the machines while he breathed in the toxic fumes of carbon tetrachloride and perchloroethylene (we called them "carbon tet" and "perc"), the chemicals that eventually killed him? He vowed that his children would never have to earn a living by the sheer sweat of their brow. Instead, we were encouraged to become teachers or lawyers or, if so inclined, writers. I never fully appreciated the opportunities I enjoyed my entire life. And it is only in retrospect, as a septuagenarian, that I realize the gift that I always had, but often wasted.

As the daughter of an immigrant, I never thought twice about the charmed life that I took for granted. I was afforded the same public education as boys, studied the violin along with my brother, and had no limitations placed upon me on how far I could go intellectually. I enjoyed a free education at the City College of New York where I later became a tenured instructor. My race, religion, and gender were never an issue. After years of procrastinating, I even published a book at the age of seventy-two, without censorship, judgment, or limitations.

* * *

Seventy-seven years after my father made his remarkable journey from Buczacz to America, nine-year-old Lev Golinkin and his family escaped from Soviet-controlled Kharkiv, Ukraine, to seek asylum in the United States. Even though Lev and my father came here decades apart, escaping from different oppressors, their families' motivation was similar - to find refuge from the religious persecution that had pervaded their cities. In 2014, Lev wrote *A Backpack, A Bear, and Eight Crates of Vodka*, a memoir about his experiences as a Soviet Jew coming to America. After reviewing his YouTube videos, magazine articles, editorials, and personal advice, I came to realize that although I was fortunate enough to be born in this great country, I had been spoiled and had taken for granted the freedoms and opportunities that had always been available to me. Lev, on the other hand, was like a dry sponge, ready to soak up all the benefits and opportunities that flow from America's spigots each and every day.

So many of us native-born Americans take our nationality for granted. Some even scorn it. Michelle Obama who, despite the obstacles she claims to have faced because of her race and gender, achieved success as an undergraduate at Princeton, a law student at Harvard, an Associate Dean of Students at the University of Chicago, and First Lady of the United States. Despite these achievements, she scoffed that she had never felt proud of her country until her husband was nominated for the presidency. On the other hand, the immigrant to whom Michelle Obama lost her job, Melania Trump, said in 2006, "I was very proud to become a citizen of the United States - the greatest privilege on planet Earth."

Why is it that those who are not blessed with being born here value being an American so much more than those of us lucky enough to have a United States birth certificate? Is it because we never experienced the stifling economic and ideological life under a dictatorship, all too often accompanied by the hardships of gender, racial, and religious discrimination? Immigrants like Lev Golinkin have taken full advantage of the opportunities afforded them here, not allowing any grass to grow under their feet. Appreciative of what he found in America, he has not wasted his time procrastinating, as I did, to achieve his goals.

My father and Lev lived a mere 792 kilometers apart in what is now Ukraine. How differently their lives evolved after coming to America! Until I corresponded with Lev Golinkin, I never fully appreciated the immigrant experience and how jaded I was. I am ashamed to admit that the thought had never entered my mind.

So, Lev Golinkin, immigrant from Kharkiv, Ukraine, and resident of New Jersey, thank you for reminding me about the blessings of being an American!

(Note: A sampling of Simon's writings can be found in the Addendum.)

PART FIVE

The Way of
All Flesh

One

Dodging the Bullet

January 27, 1995 **(journal entry)**

Something in everyone's life makes him realize his own mortality. We mosey on from day to day never expecting that we could suddenly be stopped in our tracks through no conscious fault of our own. It happens suddenly. You're feeling great, exercising, taking walks, cleaning the house, learning how to tap dance, paying bills, working, driving, laughing, having fun. The next day you feel seriously ill, wondering how you could have become so sick so quickly. Escalating blood pressure appeared almost overnight for no apparent reason, leaving me terrified that the next step I took, or the next sudden move of my head, or the next sneeze or cough would result in my having a stroke. But I was fortunate. What seemed to be a serious illness with a dreadful prognosis turned out to be reversible, caused, of all things, by ingesting too much black licorice. It reminded me of my mother's appeal to God, "Gut shrek mir, but shtrof mir nicht" ("God, frighten me, but don't punish me").

In her essay, *Three Days to See*, Helen Keller ruminates that "it would be an excellent rule to live each day as if we should die tomorrow. Such an attitude would emphasize sharply the values of life. We should live each day with a gentleness, a vigor, and a keenness of appreciation which are often lost when time stretches before us in the constant panorama of more days and months and years to come."

This essay has always had an enormous impact on me. In it, Helen Keller, who became deaf and blind at the age of eighteen months, imagines what it might be like if she had three days in which to see. She concludes that we appreciate what we have only after we have lost it. Only the blind can fully appreciate sight; only the deaf can completely comprehend the beauty of sound; and we especially value good health only when we are ill. We expect that our children will always be well and safe and never succumb to anything that might harm them. All too often we become complacent about our lives. We assume that we will always enjoy good health and doubt that we will ever face financial collapse, hoping that we will be happy forever and refusing to even think otherwise.

* * *

There is a parable that goes something like this:

An impending flood is threatening the house of a religious man who has devoted his life to God. When the flood starts to erupt, a truck comes by, and the driver tells the religious man, "Hop in. The flood is approaching." "No," replies the man of faith. "Go ahead without me. God will take care of me." The flood waters continue to rise, and a neighbor comes by in a rowboat. "Hurry. Get in!" "No" is the answer once again. "I will wait. God will save me!" So the rowboat moves on. Finally, the waters have gotten so high that the man is forced to climb up onto the roof of his house. Someone comes by in a helicopter and screams, "This is your last chance. We'll drop you a ladder. You must climb on!" "No, no. I'll be fine. God will save me." But the inevitable happens, and the religious man drowns in the flood. When he arrives in Heaven, he asks God why He didn't save him, to which God replies: "What do you mean? I sent you a truck. I sent you a rowboat. And I sent you a helicopter!"

Over the past few years, I have received many warnings. I had hemorrhagic cystitis, walking pneumonia, high blood pressure of mysterious origin, and cataract surgery followed by vitreous detachment of the retina. I kept pushing myself and plugging away, all the while worrying and getting stressed out, ignoring my inner voice that said to smell the roses, pick the daisies, take better care of myself. But now I have turned over a new leaf. God has sent me a helicopter, and I am climbing aboard!

* * *

January 2, 1993 *(journal entry)*

> *I watch my physician husband review the CT scan of a patient two days after his own near-death experience in the rough waters of the Atlantic Ocean off the coast of South Beach in Miami. Ignoring the red warning flags, he swam out into the turbulent sea. He soon realized that he was unable to catch his breath, and had it not been for the only other swimmer who had ventured out that sunny afternoon and managed to grab my husband's hand to pull him ashore, there is no doubt that he would have drowned. God had sent my husband that proverbial helicopter. Otherwise, his death would have been chalked up as just another casualty of a good swimmer overcome by Mother Nature.*

September 30, 2009 *(journal entry)*

It is a typical early fall day - cool, overcast, and breezy. Yet, while I am sitting in Starbucks enjoying my venti acai-berry green tea and organic lemon-poppy cookies, I am heavy of heart thinking about the ordeal that my cousin is facing at this very moment. She is undergoing a bilateral mastectomy to eradicate the cancer that was discovered a month ago. How quickly our peaceful lives filled with equanimity can change. In a blink of the eye, we go from contented to tormented; from happy to anxious; from complacent to fearful. I saw this so many years ago when my father, who was always slim and fit, began to feel shortness of breath, sweated profusely, and was overcome with extreme exhaustion. A blood test revealed that he had acute myeloid leukemia. Last year, my husband was diagnosed with prostate cancer.

At the time of my father's illness, I had the image in my mind that life was like a shooting duck gallery at the carnival. The metal ducks slowly rotate around and around, and the object of the game is to use a BB gun to hit one of the ducks and knock it down. I picture us all as targeted ducks going around in a circle as we try to navigate this thing called "life." Is each rotation an hour? A day? A month? A year? Some of us get shot down quickly. Others, the lucky ones, dodge the bullet aimed at us and get to go around one more time. Let us not waste the unknown number of rotations we have left. It is, after all, the roll of the dice - the luck of the draw!

* * *

*"The power of intuitive understanding will protect you from harm
until the end of your days."*

Lao Tzu (Chinese philosopher)

"The only real valuable thing is intuition."

Albert Einstein

Flashback to 1966
Cincinnati, Ohio

*Still a newlywed, I was stopped at a red light exiting our garden
apartment complex on Lakeshore Drive in Cincinnati. I was twenty-two
years old, driving our brand-new fire-engine red MGB sports coupe. Mine
was the first car waiting for the light to turn green. For some reason that
still remains a mystery to me, even after the light turned green, I hesitated
just a few seconds before proceeding to make my left turn onto Galbraith
Road. Did I subliminally hear a car horn warning me of an oncoming
car? Or, perhaps, did I subconsciously notice out of the corner of my eye a
fast-moving vehicle heading toward me? Whatever the reason might have
been, I did not accelerate immediately when the light turned green. Those
few seconds of hesitation saved my life, for as soon as I entered the inter-
section of Galbraith Road and Lakeshore Drive, a 1957 Chrysler sedan,
driven by a nurse who had been sleep-deprived after working the overnight
shift at a local hospital, came barreling down the main road at a high
rate of speed, running the red light, and colliding into my car with such
force that the entire front end, engine included, was torn completely off the
body of the car, causing the door of the passenger side to fly off its hinges.
Miraculously, except for damage to my back (which has bothered me for
the past half a century), I did not suffer any other injuries.
Talk about dodging the bullet!*

July 24, 2010 *(journal entry)*
Cherry Hill, New Jersey

    In the past week, I had two near misses (three, if you count the coughing/choking fit I experienced at the Toyota dealership). On the way to Toyota, I turned left too soon on Haddonfield Road and ended up on the must-turn left lane for the road going in the opposite direction. "Oh my God!" I whispered to myself. "This has never happened to me before." I immediately realized my mistake, and luckily, no cars were coming, so I was able to maneuver my car over the curb separating the two lanes and navigate it onto the right road. What a wake-up call! I had been feeling tired and in a funk all week, but this incident really jolted me back to reality. I started talking to myself. "Get with it!" "Stop feeling down!" "Perk up!"

    Then today, walking to the farmers market in Haddonfield, I stumbled over a high part of the sidewalk and propelled myself with small running steps until I was able to catch my balance. What a blessing not to have fallen. At sixty-six, I could have easily given in to being off-kilter, but I was determined to stay upright. A fall would have been disastrous. So whatever funk I have allowed myself to wallow in since my sixty-sixth birthday shall leave me from this moment on! Three strikes and you're out. Do I even dare to hope for nine lives?

        BE ALERT!
        NO MORE NEAR MISSES!
        DODGE THE BULLET!

Two

The Dreaded Middle of the Night Phone Call

August 24, 2020 *(journal entry)*

    It is 3:21 a.m. Somewhere in the deep recesses of my unconscious dream, a cell phone is ringing. I had deliberately chosen the ringtone "Timeless" because it has a very soothing sound, neither harsh nor alarming. But at 3:21 a.m., even "Ave Maria" would awaken me with a jolt, filling me with alarm and fear. Who could be calling at this hour? I do not want to see the area code that will tell me where the call is coming from. I am afraid it might be area code (310) - Los Angeles. Could it be the LAPD telling me that something happened to my son? Why else would they be calling me in the middle of the night? If it is (201), then it is my sister Pearl whose husband Lenny is rapidly declining in an assisted living facility in Florida, in such poor condition that he is being transferred to another facility that can better care for him. I brace myself and steal a glance at the incoming call and see that it is (850), which means that the call is coming from Tallahassee, where Steve's brother Jules is a patient in a nursing home. I mumble half to myself and half to Steve who is still asleep, "It's about Jules." It is the charge nurse at hospice, reporting that Jules is complaining of stomach pains and wants to go to the E.R.

It had been a long time since I feared being jolted out of a deep sleep by an unexpected, unwanted dreaded phone call in the middle of the night. Sparing me from what would invariably be bad news, Steve would always pick up the phone first. I worried about my chronically-ill mother, my leukemia-ridden father, and Steve's elderly mother.

But the worst call came from the Teaneck Police Department at five o'clock on a Wednesday afternoon, telling me to get over to my sister's house immediately because my nephew Steven had been killed in a car accident while speeding to the Grand Canyon to catch the sunrise. It's strange. I never get startled when I hear the phone at five in the afternoon. Only when it rings in the middle of the night.

Three

Confronting the
Unmentionable

As far back as I can remember as a child in the 1940s and 1950s and even as an adult up until the 1980s, it was strictly forbidden to even utter the word *cancer*. Because it was too horrible to verbalize, people referred to the dreaded disease as the *C word*. Perhaps that is one reason why we didn't hear about people getting cancer back then. Was it because cancer was less common or simply because no one ever mentioned it? It was, after all, "unmentionable!"

In Neil Simon's **Brighton Beach Memoirs**, Eugene talks to the audience about his uncle who has died from cancer. In his soliloquy, Eugene confides to the audience: "They always whisper it. It was (*he whispers*). . . cancer! I think they're afraid if they said it out loud, God would say, 'I HEARD THAT! YOU SAID THE DREAD DISEASE! (*He points his finger down*) JUST FOR THAT, I SMITE YOU DOWN WITH IT!!'. . ."

Eventually, society became more comfortable calling the disease by its actual name. We came to realize that the word itself was not the culprit that caused the devastating illness, and whether we called it the *C word* or *cancer*, it meant the same thing. Mentionable or unmentionable, it is real and foreboding, synonymous in our minds with a death sentence.

But it wasn't merely the *C word* that visited us that day. It was cancer itself.

* * *

October 16, 2008 7:30 a.m. *(journal entry)*
30 Kings Court, Haddonfield, NJ

So Gut **shreked** *us, but this time, He also* **shtroffed** *us. We were* **frightened***, and we were* **punished***. The call came from the urologist at 4:49 p.m. yesterday, informing us that the biopsy of Steve's prostate was positive, with the presence of cancer in two out of the twelve biopsies. Now he must undergo more tests, further treatment, and surgery. All we can do is hope for a cure.*

I think we are both in some form of denial. I know I am. Last night's sleep was broken, and I was awakened several times to the reality of the situation. Thoughts of "should have," "if only," and "what if" have drifted into my consciousness. Despite his spinal stenosis, Steve should have gone for the biopsy sooner. If only we had attended the **Kol Nidre** *service the night before Yom Kippur instead of listening to the haunting chants annulling vows made before God at home on a recording. What if we both had gone to shul (the synagogue) to be put into the* **Book of Life** *instead of praying at home. But all of this second-guessing is now moot. Steve has done tshuva (repentance), given tzedakah (charity), and engaged in tfillah (prayer), so God should be on his side.*

Once the reality has finally set in, we will proceed with what-ever needs to be done to face the biggest battle of our lives. There are to be no deals, no denials, no more "should haves," "if onlys," or "what ifs." But no matter what happens next, our lives have taken a totally different turn as of 4:49 p.m. on October 15th, 2008, and we will never be the same.

* * *

October 25, 2008 *(journal entry)*
Starbucks
Haddonfield, NJ

For the past ten days, I have been on an emotional roller coaster. We picked up the orders for a bone scan and a CT scan to see if Steve's prostate cancer metastasized to other parts of his body. Prior to his taking these tests, I was overwhelmed with anxiety. My pulse raced, my appetite waned, and I was emotionally labile. We were so thankful when both the bone scan and CT scan studies came back negative. It's funny. First, you hope that it won't be cancer. Then you pray that the cancer is confined to the prostate and are so grateful to hear that it is. How quickly we go through the stages of grief: denial, anger, bargaining, depression, and acceptance. It has been nine days, and we are getting accustomed to the diagnosis. We have no choice. We can even utter the word cancer without cringing or feeling that just by verbalizing it we are putting a whammy on ourselves, and I can now talk to people without breaking down in tears.

What happens when the healer himself becomes sick? Steve is doing everything he is supposed to do in a diligent and timely manner. At the same time, he wants us to continue doing what makes us happy - to have fun, to laugh and not be glum, even to be in denial, if that's what it takes. No morbidity, no negative thoughts, no defeatism. So I am following his lead. Mostly, he is more concerned about me than he is about himself. He even insisted I go for a massage the night before his surgery to try to relax. That is **so** Steve!

October 27, 2008 *(journal entry)*
Dining room table
Haddonfield, NJ

*Okay. So maybe I **am** angry! I keep waiting for the supportive calls, asking me, "How are you holding up?" or "How is Steve doing?" or "My thoughts are with you." So many of those calls that I crave are simply not there.*

I remember my mother feeling angry when my father had leukemia and many of those she relied on didn't reach out to her. I tried to tell her at the time that people had their own problems and family dynamics to deal with. Their lives did not revolve around her heartache. But now I realize how she felt, even though it is unrealistic and irrational. So I will shake this feeling of anger. I shall not walk around with an edge, feeling mopey all the time. People are people. It isn't comfortable dealing with someone else's problems. It's a bother, an inconvenience, a burden. I have come to the sad conclusion that it is our problem alone, and we will have to face it with love, determination, and strength.

* * *

November 9, 2008 *(journal entry)*
Starbucks - in front of the fireplace
Haddonfield, NJ

*It was on a recent episode of **House**, the popular television show that features a crotchety crippled doctor, where I first learned, in the exact order, the stages of grief outlined by Elisabeth Kübler-Ross and David Kessler in their book **On Grief and Grieving**. The stages they describe that one goes through when faced with a serious illness or another devastating life-changing event are denial, anger, bargaining, depression, and acceptance. I thought that I had passed through all of these phases,* *but now, with Steve's reprieve by postponing his surgery from October 30th to January 8th, I find that I have reverted back to denial. He did not have the surgery, so that must mean he does not have to undergo the surgery. I have come to realize that the stages are not linear. It took two weeks before I felt an overwhelming sense of anger. That was a couple of weeks ago, and I thought that I had arrived at the "acceptance" stage after we met with Steve's surgeon and felt confident in our course of action; but it did not take long before I felt an undeniable wave of sadness and depression. Kübler-Ross and Kessler oversimplified the process. I imagine that they did so with the realization that one does not move forward in a straight line but weaves back and forth from one stage to another with no discernible rhyme nor reason. Our emotions are very complex and cannot be divided into five convenient stages; and I now realize that I will invariably bounce from stage to stage with no warning or trigger that I can control or even detect.*

* * *

November 15, 2008 *(journal entry)*
Starbucks
Haddonfield, NJ

*Steve's cancer diagnosis has weighed heavily on my heart and my mind. I am awash with fear, which is conspicuously missing from Kessler and Kübler-Ross's list. Perhaps they didn't study their subjects long enough to identify this emotion, for it is only now, a month after his diagnosis, that I am beginning to experience true and unrelenting fear that rose to the surface after reading Patrick Walsh's **Surviving Prostate Cancer**. The book explained the seriousness of the diagnosis and the complexity of the surgery, along with the complications that might result. Learning about this for the first time has made me more fearful than angry or depressed. My eyes well up with tears thinking about how Steve is trying to protect **me** when it* *is **he** who must face the disease that entered his body so invasively and unexpectedly. We try to ignore it, but who can ignore the elephant in the room? We try to deny it, but how can you deny a reality that stares you in the face? And we both try so hard to quell our overwhelming fear, often without success.*

* * *

November 27, 2008 *(journal entry)*
Thanksgiving

I called my last surviving aunt to wish her a happy Thanksgiving. When she asked me how Steve was doing, I told Aunt Lilly that he wasn't afraid and that he was trying to ignore his cancer diagnosis and go on with a normal life.

"Believe me," *she said.* "He's plenty scared!"

She verbalized the unspoken fear that is not mentioned in the list of five stages. I suppose it is left out because fear is the unavoidable constant that is intertwined with all the other stages. It is forever present and never goes away.

* * *

December 23, 2008 *(journal entry)*
South Seas Hotel
Miami Beach, Florida

We are all together for a family vacation before Steve's surgery in two weeks. My dour demeanor reflects my fear and anxiety. I find myself emotionally labile, and tears well up at the slightest provocation. I tend to slouch; my writing lacks spark and spontaneity; smiling is forced; even joking has become unnatural. I no longer experience denial, bargaining, or anger. I am close to acceptance and deep into sadness. I have adopted an "I don't give a damn" attitude, filled with disinterest, nonchalance, and self-pity. I have become selfish, tinged with the bitterness I begged my mother to shed when my father was sick and people didn't call to see how she was doing.

I do not like the person I have become, so I am determined to make a serious effort to quash the negative feelings that have overtaken my normally positive persona. I will keep telling myself, "Tears, go away! Let the sun shine in. Be happy for the good run we have had and be optimistic about the future. Let positivity and happiness reign!"

* * *

January 8, 2009 *(journal entry)*
Fox Chase Cancer Center - Pre-Surgical Waiting Room

When Dr. Benardete, my tenth-grade English teacher at Spring Valley High School, had us memorize quotations from Shakespeare, I never could have guessed that I would be using "Time and the tide wait for no man" on such a monumental, life-changing day. Neither time nor the tide have waited for us, and so here it is. The day of reckoning, the day for Steve's surgery. Like it or not, ready or not, today I am forced into "acceptance," although "resignation" might be a better term.

I stayed with Steve in the pre-surgical cubicle after he met with his surgeon. Steve joked with the nurses, the anesthesiologist, and the fourth-year surgical resident, and I told him how cute he looked in his white surgical hat that looked just like a shower cap. I tried to put him in a positive frame of mind when I told him how our four-year-old granddaughter Michelle told me to "hold on tight" to the armrests as the airplane was shaking while ascending on our turbulent flight back from Miami. That image, together with the "Stand up, Grandma, and put your hand on your heart" before reciting the "Pledge of Allegiance" made him laugh so hard that he dislodged the I.V. needle from his arm. Then, just *before he was to be injected with the special cocktail that would start his journey into la-la land and the surgery beyond, Steve asked for a few minutes alone to speak to his Maker. Steve got teary-eyed only when Emily left his side and he could see the worry and concern on his daughter's face. More concerned about me than about himself, he insisted that I go to yoga and get a massage yesterday when he saw how stressed and anxious I was. After returning from my massage, I announced that I was now ready for his surgery!*

Once Steve was wheeled into the operating room, I retreated to what they call the Quiet Room. It is here that I have been pouring out my thoughts, thankful to those who called yesterday to wish Steve good luck and are praying for a good surgical outcome. And now, it is in Dr. Greenberg's and God's hands. May God look kindly upon a man filled with so much love and virtue, and may He give Dr. Greenberg the tools he needs to perform a successful operation.

Two-and-a-half hours into the surgery with at least another three hours to go, I whisper aloud, "Steve, know how much I love you and pray that you are doing well. Remember to hold on tight!"

* * *

January 20, 2009 **(journal entry)**
Dr. Greenberg's office

Twelve days post-op, we returned to Dr. Greenberg's office to have the catheter removed and to find out the results of the surgery and the pathology report. Neither of us spoke about what was foremost in our minds, but internally, I knew we were both apprehensive. I asked myself, "If the pathology report was good, why hadn't the doctor called to alleviate our fears?" We tried to comfort each other by saying how grateful we were to have at least reached this point in our uphill journey.

The moment Dr. Greenberg entered the examining room, I

was hoping he would blurt out, "Great news, everything was fine!" But he didn't. Instead he inquired, "How are you doing? Any problems?" **"Out with it!"** I wanted to shout.

"How's the pathology report?" Steve inquired matter-of-factly, as though he was asking about the lab results of one of his patients, not his own.

Finally, we heard the news that we dared not anticipate. "The cancer was present in both lobes, but the Gleason was six, not seven as originally thought. The margins were clear, and the lymph nodes were negative."

What a relief! "Thank God," was all I could say.

I was extremely grateful, but I did not know how to react to the good news. I felt as though I had been involved in a near-miss accident when we are strong and brave during the event only to fall apart, shaken and weak following the incident. The total exhaustion while keeping up a cheerful and optimistic front and the excessive energy needed to hold things together all unravelled, and on the third day after Steve's post-op appointment, I totally lost it. Similar to postpartum depression, I cried at the drop of a hat and felt sorry for myself. I don't know what came over me. How selfish of me. But the kettle had boiled over, and I could not stop the flow. I had reached my saturation point, and all of the anxiety, fear, worry, anger, and frustration just bubbled over.

It did not take long for these feelings to pass, replaced by exhilaration that Steve had indeed beaten the dreaded C word! He had dodged the bullet.

Four

Disappointment Vs
Devastation

September 2, 2009 *(journal entry)*
Haddonfield, NJ

    What a glorious day! No humidity, temperature in the mid-70s, slight breeze and sunny. A gorgeous late summer day. A great day to be alive!

    For almost the entire month of August, I was laid up with what was probably pneumonia - although our best friend John (still a practicing physician) said there was a resurgence of whooping cough in adults whose vaccine had worn off long ago. Whatever it was, I am grateful that it responded to Zithromax; and when people sympathize about my being out of commission for a month, I tell them that I am just happy that I had something that was treatable. So what if I lost a month of summer, missing out on swimming a few times a week or taking long walks in the park or going to the beach. As my mother used to say, "The mensch tracht und Gut lacht" ("People make plans and God laughs!").

My first outing was to Atlantic City with Steve for a big poker tournament. He made it to number 24 out of 210 players, only three away from coming into the money. He felt terrible and disappointed when his pocket kings didn't hold up after he went all-in and a guy with a big chip stack called with an ace-six. When an ace came out on the river, Steve was eliminated from the tournament, leaving him feeling defeated and devastated. He had played really good poker for fifteen and a half hours, starting at 11:00 a.m. until 2:30 the following morning. It took him several days to get over it.

However, these things must be put into their proper perspective.

de-vas-ta-tion: severe and overwhelming shock or grief.
"She spoke of her devastation at his death."

dis-ap-point-ment: sadness or displeasure caused by the non-fulfillment of one's hopes or expectations.
"To her disappointment, she did not get the job."

Devastation is when your mother has a dissecting aortic aneurysm and you know she is going to die in a matter of hours; or when your father is so debilitated by his leukemia that all you can do is swab the inside of his mouth with medicated Q-tips to relieve the pain of the sores from his chemotherapy treatment; or when your husband and partner and love of your life is told that he has cancer. Reminding ourselves of these terrible situations makes us realize that losing with pocket kings is a joke! There will always be another tournament to stoke our excitement and enthusiasm. Hope springs eternal! But there are no do-overs with death or awful diagnoses. How fortunate we are to be able to sign up for a new poker tournament and start all over again!

PART SIX

Such is Life

One

Life and the Weather

A METAPHOR

June 24, 2003 *(journal entry)*
SS Carnival Victory
Atlantic Ocean -somewhere between New York City
and Nova Scotia

*I am sitting on the tenth deck of the **SS Carnival Victory**
heading toward Nova Scotia, Canada. There is a brisk wind, chilling the
summer air. The fog is dense. There is zero visibility. Even the ocean is
obscure. The captain slowly sounds the deafening fog horn five seconds at a
time. There is no panic to the intensity and frequency of the horn's whistle,
for it is merely indicating the ship's position and alerting other craft that
our ship is nearby. The captain casually announces that the sea is two
thousand feet deep.*
I am on the brink, the edge, the cusp of my fifty-ninth birthday.

*The clarity of my future is like the fog into which the **Victory** is entering. Even the name Victory can be compared to my life. I have been blessed with a wonderful husband; I have enjoyed good health; I have loving children and precious grandchildren. Life is good. Approaching my sixth decade, heading into the thick fog and hearing the warning whistles by the captain of the **Victory**, I reflect on my own past victories, yet anticipate with some trepidation the uncertain fog I am likely to encounter.*

* * *

September 16, 2003 *(journal entry)*
Spring Lake, New Jersey
sitting on the beach - noon

The sea is calm until it nears the shore where three-foot waves crash, spraying up the turbulent ocean water. Hurricane Isabel is not expected to arrive for another two days, but already hotels are boarded up and outdoor furniture is being secured. Right now, the sun is shining, and the ocean is serene. It is the calm before the storm.

I try to write, but the fountain that was once filled with words so overflowing that my hand could not keep up with my thoughts as I rushed to write what was in my mind lest I forget is now quiet and depleted. How can that be? Have all my thoughts been written? Or are there ideas filled with energy mounting within me just as the impending storm is building to a crescendo and will climactically burst forth with uncontrollable speed and unbridled force?

* * *

February 26, 2004 *(journal entry)*
7:11 a.m.
Aboard the **Norwegian Sun** cruise ship

I am watching the sunrise from the aft of the ship. It is the rebirth of a new day, a beautiful affirmation of life, just one more reason to be thankful for being alive. This is in contrast to the choppy seas that are causing chairs to slide across the deck and dishes to fly off tables. We are heading toward Costa Maya, Mexico, feeling the effects of a storm in Texas on this, the fourth day of our Caribbean cruise.

The whole dichotomy of a radiant sunrise and threatening seas is a metaphor of life itself - the beauty and expectation of life anew, peppered with the inevitable ups and downs that life has in store for each of us. It is that affirmation of life and the comfort of knowing that the sun will rise each day that makes my spirit soar and revitalizes my soul. As the new day dawns, there is renewed hope and promise for all things good.

Two

Strife while Striving Desperately to "Smell the Roses"

May 28, 1999 *(journal entry)*
5:00 a.m.

  My dreams have been vivid, reflecting my vulnerability and loss of control. They are so unsettling that I am unable to shake their images from my mind for hours after I awaken. I dream that no matter how hard I try, I cannot memorize the lines of a play; I have difficulty following the recipe, and the cake collapses; I don't take proper care of the baby; the office is disorganized, and I am unable to make appointments on the right days; I defecate in public; my feet cannot quite reach the pedals of the car, and my hands can't grasp the steering wheel. I wake up sweating, whether from fear or from menopause, I cannot say; and then I hear the sounds of birds singing. The songbirds are beautiful as they, too, wake up from a night of rest, hovering over the rose bushes in bloom. It is a metaphor of life itself: "Wake up and smell the roses." Throughout the busy years of raising children, working, taking care of a house, building a marriage and a medical practice, I never gave myself enough time to listen to the birds call to each other or watch the flowers grow. Hopefully, as the years advance, I will eventually come to appreciate and become more cognizant of the wonderful miracles around me. I cannot wait to wake up in time to smell the roses.

* * *

August 21, 2000 *(journal entry)*
Bergenfield, NJ

I am sitting under an oak tree, admiring my beautiful flower garden. With a smile on my face, I drink in the black-eyed Susans - bright yellow flowers with dark brown centers - growing amidst the huge hibiscus. I call the hibiscus "crepe-paper flowers" because they remind me of the flowers I made using brightly colored crepe paper when I was a child. My eyes move to the butterfly bush, where a monarch butterfly has taken its cue and landed on one of the pink blossoms, its orange and black wings fluttering softly in the breeze. Harmless bumblebees surround the Fairy roses, while fragrant red roses lazily climb up the white picket fence. The giant hostas bearing lily white flowers adorn the garden where they stand majestically on thick, sturdy stalks. Crows flap their wings as though they are actors in an animated film, upstaged by the squirrels who shake their tails while perched on the fence posts eating their lunch of acorns and pine cones. Everything seems so Disneyesque that I want to break out in song, "It's a lovely day today!" Occasionally, a robin or a cardinal or a sparrow unhurriedly flies around the property, who, like me, is reluctant to leave, choosing to remain within the confines of the garden and relishing in its *beauty. What peace I find in my small but bountiful garden surrounding my charming cottage built in 1931!*

Can it be that I have begun to smell the roses?

Three

On Change

The anticipation of change, not necessarily change itself, has always been my nemesis. Looking back objectively, I realize that I never liked change, but eventually, I managed to adjust to it. When Steve decided to leave his successful, stable career to go to medical school, I felt an enormous level of anxiety at the thought of becoming the sole breadwinner. When we moved to Spanish Harlem in New York City, I accepted my new role as college professor, wife of a medical student, and soon after, a mother, with grace and equanimity. We relocated twice within a short period of time, first to Edgewater, New Jersey, and then, in 1973, to nearby Teaneck. I do not recall much trepidation prior to those two moves; but in 1980, when we purchased a large house on an acre of property fourteen miles away in Allendale, I was very apprehensive about the changes in my life that the move would incur. The house would be a greater financial burden; the children would be uprooted from their schools and their friends; and I would be stuck in an isolated area where

I didn't know a soul. Picking Todd up from his first day of sixth grade at Brookside School confirmed my worst fears when I was greeted with tears streaming down his face and a running monologue of why he didn't like it there, culminating with "... *and I have to take French!*"

We were settled into our new environment when three years later, we were faced with a change that was totally out of our control. My father, a fit healthy man of seventy-three, was diagnosed with acute leukemia. Death, the final and the hardest change of all, came knocking on my father's door in 1984. Eight months later, our family was reeling with the untimely death of my loving nephew, Steven, leaving a permanent indelible hole in our hearts. Unexpected change that brings tragedy and heartache puts the nonsensical anxiety that we feel when we *choose* change into the proper perspective.

I have welcomed natural lifetime changes, finding profound joy in milestones that have shaped my life - the births of my children and grandchildren; graduations from high school and college; engagements and weddings. Todd's change from being a secular intellectual to becoming a black-hat Orthodox rabbi affected us all in a positive way, although I must admit, it took a while to get used to his new lifestyle. Emily got engaged, and Jeff moved to Germany to edit a film. In 1998, we moved from our big house in Allendale to a charming cottage in Bergenfield just two blocks from our first home in Teaneck. We had come full circle. Unlike the move to Allendale eighteen years earlier, I welcomed this change and soon came to love my new surroundings, setting up house with lace curtains and antique furnishings in all the nooks and crannies of our 1931 refurbished and restored cottage surrounded by a white picket fence within which Steve created a wonderful fairy-tale garden that I loved.

It was not long before managed care imposed so many draconian constraints and limitations upon Steve's ability to practice medicine in the exceptional manner to which he was accustomed that we were unable to meet our expenses and were forced to close our medical office. In 2006, we simultaneously made three major changes that have been described as the most difficult and stressful in one's lifetime. We sold our house and put our belongings into storage; we gave up our livelihood, retiring from our medical practice of over thirty years; and we got on the road for what was to become a nine-month road trip around the country. These changes were both stressful and exciting. Only once during our road trip adventure did I succumb to the overwhelming stress I felt because of the change in direction our lives had taken. I will share my thoughts here for the first time as I recorded them in a motel room in Albuquerque, New Mexico.

October 25, 2006 *(journal entry)*

After seventy-two days on the road, I finally succumbed to the anxieties and uncertainties I had been keeping in check since we started on our road trip. At 8:23 a.m., getting ready to leave our motel room, stating that I did not want to speed because the pavement was wet after a night of heavy rain, I was accused of being negative. That was all it took for the myriad of emotions I had kept buried since we embarked on the road trip to rise to the surface and explode.

I entered the bathroom and began to weep uncontrollably. "What have I done? Why did I ever agree to this road trip? Why did we sell the house we loved?" After allowing myself a brief outburst by myself and for myself, I got dressed and am now ready to go. Will this be the start of expressing my true feelings not camouflaged by the Pollyanna-like, sugar-coated entries in my journal? I kept promising myself that "I wouldn't go there" whenever I was plagued by regretful thoughts of giving up my home and leaving on this road trip. Perhaps suppressing my innermost feelings wasn't a wise thing to do. But my forte has always been to adjust to different situations and try to put a positive spin on change. Schizophrenically, it seems that I react over-positively to change while negative feelings are percolating just under the surface.

NOTE: Looking back, it turns out that the road trip was one of our most memorable and meaningful experiences; giving up the medical practice made the most financial and practical sense; and selling our house so that we could eventually live near our daughter and her family was definitely a good decision.

So change, while often uncomfortable, even painful, usually works out for the best.

Four

On Gambling

They stand like mannequins, posed in disbelief or frustration, elation or mild embarrassment, as the escalator brings them from the casino floor to the outside where they will get into their cars to escape the tentacles of the gaming tables. Mesmerized by the intoxication of the over-oxygenated, heavily air-conditioned atmosphere where there is no day or night, no summer or winter, no spring or fall, they exit like robots to return to their homes where reality sets in and a dollar is a dollar and not a white chip you carelessly toss into the tray of a scantily clad waitress who brings you a complimentary bottle of water.

Sometimes they argue openly over losing the rent money, while the loser sheepishly cowers to the rantings of the more disciplined, perhaps luckier, partner. In the elevator, they stand glaring at each other with anger so deep that it is clear that they did not have a good day; or, arms around each other, they celebrate their victory without uttering a word. Once, I heard an elderly woman shouting into her cell phone over the din of the casino noise that she had won ten *thousand* dollars in a slot machine jackpot.

While looking for a parking space in the garage of the casino, I almost collided with a speeding car going in the wrong direction driven by a young man anxious to get the hell out of there. And there are stories of desperate gamblers who have lost everything, including their lives, when they felt they had no choice but to jump off a nearby bridge.

My father was wont of saying that the thrill he experienced when he won at gambling never made up for how bad he felt when he lost. It is a word to the wise.

Five

On Saving

I came up with a great idea of opening a savings account wherein I would deposit any money that I made on proceeds from stuff I brought to consignment shops, money I did not spend for things I really did not need, and any winnings at poker. I decided to do this a few days ago, but so far, I haven't been too successful.

Take the pen I am using now, for example. Just because the sign said, "Life is too short to use an ugly pen," did it mean that I had to have the *Spimoni Retro 1951* marbleized gel pen for $28.95 plus $12.95 for the refills I purchased at *The Paper Trail* stationary store right here in Haddonfield? That would have been $41.90 in the bank. What about the vinyl flowered Vera Bradley gardening tote bag with nine outside pockets I just purchased at **Serendipity of Haddonfield** for $43.66? The hot pink *Hot Cotton* shirt and silk Nieman Marcus designer scarf at **Contact Exchange Consignment Shop** would have brought the account balance to $85.56, and the *Regatta Stuhrling Original* waterproof watch at the same shop for $39.44 would have brought it up to a cool one hundred and twenty-five bucks!

I must admit, though, that I love writing with the new pen; the shirt and scarf match the Vera Bradley bag perfectly; and the watch (that lists for $350.00) has been on my wrist ever since I got it four days ago. So rather than beat myself up for spending all this money on things I did not need, I will chalk it up as a continuation of my birthday celebration last week and enjoy using everything I bought.

Perhaps I will do better once I open up the account. Then I will scour my closets and drawers to find items to consign; I will resist compulsive shopping; and I will play a tighter game of *Texas Hold'em* and win at poker. I am determined to put the money I save from now on into my new quarter of a percent interest-yielding savings account that I plan to open up tomorrow!

Six

On Gratitude

"I cried because I had no shoes until I met a man who had no feet."
Persian Proverb

"Only the deaf appreciate hearing, only the blind realize the manifold blessings that lie in sight."
Helen Keller

June 25, 2016 **(journal entry)**
Starbucks
Cherry Hill, NJ

It is no coincidence that I tend to reflect on being grateful for good health around the time of my birthday. When I can chalk up another year during which I have managed to dodge the bullet, I realize just how fortunate I am to have arrived at yet another birthday. After I woke up at 6:30 a.m. to a serenade of birds singing, I cleaned the shower *(because I could), changed the dining room tablecloth (because I could), and walked the quarter mile to Starbucks for my free birthday beverage, a venti latte with coconut milk (because I could). At seventy-two, I am feeling great and grateful for my physical and mental good health, grateful for my fifty plus years of marriage to my one and only soul mate, grateful for my children and grandchildren. I am grateful for just being alive!*

*Yesterday, I did restorative yoga (because I could) with my fifteen-year-old granddaughter Aviva and spent the rest of the day with her little sister Amy, who just turned six. In celebration of her birthday, the two of us went to **The Picket Fence Tea House** in Haddonfield, where she poured her hot chocolate into a tiny porcelain teacup, used pincers to drop a sugar cube into her cup, and then carefully stirred the mixture of sugar, hot chocolate, and mini-marshmallows before elegantly sipping the concoction with her pinky in the air! Watching her and listening to her running commentary on what she was doing made me realize how fortunate I am to have this wondrous relationship not only with her but with her sisters as well. So today, I plan to follow my usual routine, including writing in my journal and going to the JCC pool to lounge and read and swim - all because at seventy-two, I still can!*

Tomorrow, we will drive to Scranton to celebrate our oldest grandchild Sarah's high school graduation. I can't believe that the baby in the ICU in Baltimore when she was six months old is graduating from high school. It seems like only yesterday that we received Todd's concerned telephone call because tiny Sarah was whimpering and breathing funny. Steve diagnosed the gravity of her condition over the telephone and told Todd to get her to the hospital immediately and insist on seeing an intensivist. We jumped in the car and made it to Baltimore from Allendale in record time, driving at ninety-five miles per hour (resulting in a year of panic attacks whenever I drove fast). Steve saved her life, and now we will get to celebrate her high school graduation.

We are doing well. I would like our finances to be more secure, but I refuse to look down the abyss. As Steve says, doing so will just suck us in. *I am grateful and I am happy to want what I have. I know that life can change in a flash. My oldest cousin fell, fracturing her leg, arm, and shoulder. Another cousin's husband, who has suffered from multiple sclerosis for decades, has taken a turn for the worse and is now unable to use his hands that he relied on to use the computer, which was his lifeline to the outside world. Two people in my weight-loss program have cancer, one metastatic. I look back at my own mother at my age, laden with the disabilities associated with her unrelenting rheumatoid arthritis.*

So , yes. I am grateful. I am most grateful!

Seven

The Unity of Humankind

"The first cry of a newborn baby in Chicago or Zamboanga, in Amsterdam or Rangoon, has the same pitch and key, each saying, "I am! I have come through! I belong! I am a member of the Family!"
Carl Sandburg (Prologue to *The Family of Man*)

During the course of my travels, the sameness of people everywhere never ceases to amaze me. When we dock at an island early in the morning, I love to look out from the ship's deck and marvel at the hustle and bustle of rush hour, so similar in many ways to rush hour in other places I know. Cars and trucks can be seen on the distant roads winding up and down the mountains, while small boats scurry around the harbor, navigated by captains whose job it is to move people or goods from place to place. There is a familiarity to the dawn of a new day, whether on the island of Manhattan or the island of Tortola. In each place, children are abruptly awakened from a peaceful slumber and grudgingly get ready for school. Universally, fathers and mothers get up, prepare breakfast, and either leisurely or frenetically leave for work in cars or trucks; or they go on foot to their jobs on the piers, in tourist shops, at factories, or in offices. Manhattan and Tortola are about the same size (22.82 square miles for Manhattan and 21.5 square miles for Tortola) but have vastly different populations of 1.6 million vs twenty-four thousand, respectively. But no matter the size or population, life on these two islands are more similar than different when it comes to the morning rush. It is a constant reminder to me that we are all members of the same Family of Man.

PART SEVEN

Women of Valor

Strength and dignity are her clothing;
She laughs at the time to come.
She opens her mouth with wisdom;
And the law of kindness is on her tongue.

(*Eshet Ḥayil* Book of Proverbs, 31)

One

To Esther Anderman

IN MEMORIAM

My grandmother, Esther Anderman (nee Nierenberg), was widowed at the age of thirty-eight. Left with five children, my father being the youngest, she was forced into the role of single mother long before it was a demographic. My father idolized and revered his mother. He made few requests of his own three children, but he asked each of us to honor his mother by naming our first daughters after her. That is why there are so many women on our side of the Anderman family with names starting with the letter "E". Her first namesake was *Etta*, the daughter of my father's first cousin Philip Nierenberg. Then came the great-granddaughters she never knew. There is Fay's *Alise Esther*, Siggy's *Elissa*, Pearl's *Elena*, and my own daughter *Emily*, all of whom bear the Hebrew name *Esther*.

It is the custom of Ashkenazi Jews to name a child after a relative who has passed away. In so doing, both the name and the memory of the departed loved one are kept alive, and in a metaphysical way, forms a bond between the soul of the baby and the person after whom she is named. This is a great honor to the deceased because its soul can achieve an elevation based on the good deeds of the namesake, while the child will be inspired by the good qualities of the deceased and have a deep connection to the past.

The naming of a Jewish child is a most profound spiritual moment. The Sages say that naming a baby is a statement of her character, her specialness, and her path in life, for at the beginning of life we receive a name, and at the end of life a good name is all we take with us (*Talmud – Brachot 7b; Arizal – Sha'ar HaGilgulim 24b*).

It is no coincidence that my grandmother carried the name of Queen Esther, the heroine of the Purim story. Esther Nierenberg Anderman was blessed with the same initiative, faith, and courage as the Esther whose name she bore. Like Queen Esther, who saved the Jewish people, my grandma Esther saved us Andermans through her own initiative, faith, and courage by coming to America and starting a new life.

I have been trying to piece together the conditions in Buczacz that prompted my grandmother Esther to leave the only life she had ever known to make the long and arduous journey to America. Buczacz was a renowned religious center, boasting The Great Synagogue, which was as lush and lavish in its ornate fixtures and furnishings as it was in its rich source of Jewish learning. Adjacent to the synagogue was The Old Study House, a Jewish learning center overflowing with Jewish texts of the Babylonian and Jerusalem Talmud as well as tomes filled with topics ranging from astronomy and engineering to mathematics and history. Interspersed with the multitude of books dealing with a plethora of different topics, there were books on grammar and a large collection of dictionaries.

There was a dichotomy between the constant fear of the organized massacres aimed at the destruction or annihilation of the Jews and the complacency felt by the large population of Jewish scholars who found comfort in their Jewish environs and whose main goal was to preserve the rich history of Judaism. My grandfather, Alexander Zisha, along with many other Jewish religious scholars, was adamantly opposed to leaving Buczacz, fearing that doing so would lead to acculturation and assimilation. Others, like my grandmother Esther, felt equally as motivated in their desire to emigrate to America. I can only conjecture the extent to which my grandparents disagreed about leaving Buczacz. My grandfather's argument must have been more compelling because in addition to his firm religious beliefs, he was chronically and terminally ill with advanced kidney disease. His declining health, combined with his deep religious convictions, probably convinced my grandmother that it was better to remain in Buczacz, even though it was riddled with anti-Semitism perpetuated by the pogroms targeting the Jewish community and sanctioned by the government.

Anti-Semitic sentiment was pervasive. As described by Omer Bartov in his book *Anatomy of a Genocide: The Life and Death of a Town Called Buczacz*, "Jewish moneylenders, shop and tavern keepers, cattle dealers [my ancestors' livelihood], estate and mill leasers or owners were all presented as fleecing the ignorant peasants, tricking them into alcohol and tobacco addiction, lending them money at cutthroat rates."

In one local newspaper, *Batkivshchyna (Fatherland)*, there was a special section dedicated to reports by local activists in Galician villages. Bartov describes "villages where out of a hundred households it is hard to find a single landed peasant who is not in debt - to the Jews, of course." Another report asserted that once a peasant borrows money from a Jew he "can't get the Jew off his back; he pays and works off the debt, but still ends up losing his land." Jews were blamed for "crushing out all artistic sense in the peasants by supplanting their really good handiwork with the vilest machine-made trash that he can procure."

Having completed a fourth-grade education, Esther was able to read the hateful anti-Semitic articles in her local Buczacz newspapers and was no stranger to the anti-Semitism spewed by her non-Jewish neighbors. Once Alexander Zisha died, there was no longer a reason to remain in Buczacz, so it is no surprise that my grandmother booked her passage in steerage on *The Amerika* soon after the death of her forty-one-year-old husband. She had seen the handwriting on the wall and was now a free agent to escape from Buczacz by fulfilling her dream of emigrating to America. It was her foresight, bravery, and steadfast determination that guaranteed the preservation of our branch of the Anderman family tree.

Planning for the grueling trip in steerage from Hamburg to America must have been daunting. She had to choose which of her children would come with her, and after careful consideration, she decided to bring along my father, who was the baby, and Rose, who was nine years old. She left behind eight-year-old Sophie and her oldest son Joseph, both of whom joined their family in America the following year. Sophie and Joseph were passengers on the last ship to leave Hamburg for New York before the outbreak of the First World War.

In 1913, the average cost of a ticket in steerage was thirty dollars for the voyage to New York. Without telephones, email, Facebook, or other media that might have prepared Esther for the horrible conditions that awaited her on *The Amerika*, there was no way of predicting what the conditions in steerage would be like. While I never heard a first-hand account from my grandmother on her transatlantic passage, I can only assume that it was not unlike that of another eyewitness passenger, Sadie Frowne, who wrote about her 1905 voyage to America in steerage:

"We came by steerage on a steamship in a very dark place that smelt dreadfully. There were hundreds of other people packed in with us, men, women, and children, and almost all of them were sick. There was no clean air, no privacy, and the food was awful. It took us twelve days to cross the sea, and we thought we should die, but at last the voyage was over, and we came up and saw the beautiful bay and the big woman with the spikes on her head and the lamp that is lighted at night in her hand."

Esther was passenger #100796061185 on *The Amerika* which departed on November 6, 1913, from Hamburg, Germany, stopping at Southampton, England, and Cherbourg, France, before arriving in New York City on November 15, 1913. In the Registry Room at Ellis Island, she had to deny being either a polygamist or an anarchist. It was documented that she was five feet, five inches tall, with black hair, brown eyes, and no marks of identification. It was further noted that she was neither deformed nor crippled, her mental and physical health were good, and her complexion was fair. She declared that the amount of money she had in her possession was eighty dollars and told the authorities at Ellis Island that she was going to live with her daughter, Sarah, at 155 Norfolk Street in New York City.

Esther had lived her entire life in Buczacz, a town centered in a crater between two plateaus, surrounded by mountains and dotted with valleys, forests, and farms. The main street and the marketplace were situated at the lower part of the valley, and houses were built along the surrounding slopes. Bridges spanned across the picturesque Strypa River that flowed through the entire town. Esther gave up living in this bucolic setting for the foul odors, invasive noise, filth, and squalor of the streets on the Lower East Side of Manhattan. My father remembered that there was no central heat and that the toilet was in the yard. He recalled coming home one day excited that his mother had gotten him a pet cat. Except it wasn't a pet cat. It turned out to be a huge water rat, the size of a cat!

New York was not the *golden medine* that Esther had envisioned - the golden state where money was said to grow on trees and a Jew could make a decent living. Nor did she escape anti-Semitism when she came to New York City. Instead of organized pogroms with their Russian and Polish troublemakers, it was the New York City policemen who looked the other way when Irish and Italian hooligans chased my father with the intent of beating him for his role in killing Christ, their savior.

It must have been so comforting for Esther to discover **The Forward** (**The Forverts**) when she arrived in New York City. Written in Yiddish, she was able to read comments by like-minded immigrants trying to make sense of their new lives in America. She was especially drawn to the Jewish advice column called **A Bintel Brief**. She read letters by men who were betrayed by their wives and by women whose husbands cheated on them. She read about the tragedy of a young woman saved from the Triangle Shirtwaist Factory fire by her beloved husband who perished trying to save the lives of other young workers trapped in that horrific fire on March 15, 1911. Parents lamented about the assimilation and acculturation that the Buczacz religious scholars warned against. Underlying many of the letters were the struggles of newly-arrived immigrants who, like herself, were trying to adjust to their new way of life and eke out a living in an overcrowded job market. But the stories of others paled in comparison to what my grandmother had endured. Her story rivaled the problems she read about in **A Bintel Brief**. She herself was not immune to great suffering and heartache. If she had written to the editor of **A Bintel Brief**, her letter might have looked something like this:

(*Note: This letter and response from the editor are figments of the author's imagination. The facts, however, are real.*)

February 21, 1918

Dear Mr. Editor,

I read your column every day. I am a 43-year-old widow. I came here to *the golden medine* five years ago after my husband died. He studied Torah all day, but G-d could not save him from the kidney failure he suffered from. I came here with my baby, Shimshee, and my beautiful daughter Rose. The following year, I was able to send for my other two children, Sophie and Joseph. My daughter, Sarah, already was here. She is a real pioneer. When she was sixteen, she sent for a ticket to come here without telling me so she could work as a dress designer in New York. She would have been scorned if she became a seamstress in Buczacz. It wasn't what a respectable young woman did. We moved in with her in her apartment on Norfolk Street. She is now seventeen. Yesterday, I buried my beautiful fourteen-year-old daughter Rose. Thank G-d for the Hebrew Free Burial Society who made the burial possible at the Mount Richmond Cemetery on Staten Island. The doctor said she bled to death from her stomach. I am so heartbroken. A year after we came here, my son Joseph went to the beach at Coney Island. It was so hot that day, and I was so happy that he was going to enjoy a day at the beach. He decided to jump off the Steeplechase Pier to swim in the ocean at Coney Island. It gave him an ear infection. He died from it. The doctors called it a mastoid. He was fifteen. *Baruch Hashem* I still have my Shimshee (they call him Simon in school). He is eight years old and the light of my life. He loves school. The teachers tell me he is very smart. Sophie is thirteen. She left school and works as a seamstress like her sister Sarah, who is my rock. Without them, I don't know what I would do. The streets where we live are very noisy and crowded and dirty. Sophie came home the other day and was so excited that I got her a pet cat. Only it wasn't a cat. It was a great big rat! Simon, now the man of the house, chased it away with a broom. I am not complaining about how we live. It is better than what we faced in Buczacz, where the anti-Semitism was all over the place. I am just so heartbroken and I hope I will be able to cope with the loss of my two wonderful children. Did I mention that two of my little boys died in Europe? So life has been hard. I hope to one day have grandchildren to brighten my life. Thank you for hearing my tale of woe.

Respectfully, Esther Anderman

Answer from the Editor:

Dear Esther Anderman,

My heart breaks when I hear the suffering and heartache you have. Please be strong. I am confident that you will find happiness and *nachas* from your remaining children and future grandchildren. Remember that you are the namesake of a very strong woman who saved the Jewish people through strength, initiative, faith, and courage. *Zei Gezunt* (be well).

* * *

And blessings did, indeed, eventually rain upon her. Her children married and had children of their own. Sarah remained childless, but Sophie had two children, Fay and Cecile; and Simon had three, Pearl, Sigmund Alexander (named for her beloved husband), and myself, Carol Rila (named after her daughter, Rose). Her children moved her from the squalor of a tenement on the Lower East Side to an apartment in Williamsburg, Brooklyn. After Sophie's husband died, she moved in with her family and became a second mother to Fay and Cecile. She spent summers with us in Spring Valley, where she taught us how to knit and play *pisha paysha*.*

When I was a young child, she was just "Grandma." I never really thought about her in terms of where she came from or the trials and tribulations she had suffered. She died at the age of seventy-four, just before I turned eight. It is only on the reflections of this septuagenarian that I can fully appreciate the sacrifices, courage, and foresight that Esther possessed, making it possible for her branch of the Anderman family not only to have survived, but to have thrived.

So here's to my grandmother, Esther Anderman, *In Memoriam*.

---

* A card game for two players one of whom is usually a child, wherein the deck is placed face down with one card facing upward. Players draw from the deck alternately hoping to build up or down from the open card. So, for instance, if there is an 8, the opponent can put on a 7 or a 9, and so on. The player with no remaining cards is the winner.

Two

Rosie and Women's Lib (two generations of liberated women)

Coming of age in the 1960s at the dawn of the women's movement, I was lectured by feminists like Betty Friedan and Gloria Steinem that women were considered weak and subservient to men and that it was about time for women to become liberated. What I did not realize was that I had been blessed with a strong woman not only in my midst, but in my very household. She was my mother Rosie!

Long before it was in vogue, my mother was truly liberated. She worked outside the home, staunchly protected her children, and remained a devoted wife and immaculate homemaker, all the while heroically fighting the multitude of physical ailments that ravaged her body. It was Rosie's Herculean efforts and indomitable spirit that allowed her to maintain her independence well into her eighties, while others with similar disabilities were confined to wheelchairs or strapped to hospital gurneys.

Rosie was a strong woman, not because she marched in protests or signed petitions because she never did, warning us never to sign a petition. (She had learned her lesson after my father once signed a petition in support of The Workmen's Circle, an organization founded in 1900 that acted as a mutual aid society to help Jewish immigrants adapt to their new life in America. Decades later, when my father applied for a job with New York State, the petition he had signed surfaced, and because The Workmen's Circle was considered a subversive organization, my father was denied employment. He had to appeal, and was ultimately able to get the job.) Instead of overtly protesting, Rosie demonstrated her strength by teaching us, through example, the resilience, perseverance, and power of women. I don't think she realized it, but she was truly a women's libber! But unlike many others who described themselves as such, she neither hated men nor considered them her enemies. In fact, she did not find it necessary for a strong woman to discard her femininity. She sported her bright red nail polish, rouge, and eyebrow pencil, making her as beautiful as she was strong.

* * *

April 8, 2008 *(journal entry)*

Three days after what would have been her 92nd birthday, I recall Rosie's remedies.

Nobody could take out a splinter as painlessly as my mother. The moment we reported our affliction to Rosie, she immediately dropped whatever she was doing and began preparing for the removal of the foreign object. First, she dissolved a tablespoon of boric acid powder in a glass of lukewarm water where the affected finger or toe was to be soaked. While this process was taking place, Rosie would take down her sewing box and remove a sewing needle. This was to be the instrument for extraction - but not until it was sterilized by striking a match and holding the lighted flame under the needle for several seconds. Anxiously awaiting the impending operation, the afflicted child would nervously flit his or her eyes from the wound to my mother, while the other two siblings looked on with wonder and expectation. Our fear was appeased the moment my mother carefully held the splinter-inhabited finger in her small frail hand. Although deformed from her rheumatoid arthritis, my mother's fingers were still limber enough to hold the sterilized needle in her right hand, while her left hand gently, but firmly, held the operative site. With her yet unimpaired vision, she isolated the area in which the splinter was lodged and ever so gingerly poked around the splinter, lifting up the surrounding skin that had been softened by the soaking solution. When the entire splinter was finally exposed, Rosie used a tweezer that had been sterilized in the same manner as the needle to grasp the splinter at just the perfect angle so it would not break into small pieces. The patient and observers all watched as the gruesome procedure was performed, amazed that such an extraction was so painless. One of the onlookers was then instructed to fetch the iodine from the medicine cabinet. The last step was applying the iodine to the area now sans splinter, followed by the best part of all - my mother's kiss!

* * *

What are you supposed to do when you are sitting at a table and someone begins to choke? Whether a crumb got caught in our throat, a sip of juice went down the wrong pipe, or a piece of chicken went down the wrong way, Rosie's remedy was to exclaim, "HANDS UP!" Immediately, the choking victim would quickly raise up his or her hands and hold them there until the coughing/choking fit stopped. And, like magic, it always worked!

Oil of Wintergreen was the remedy for sore muscles; boric acid solution was used to soak an infected finger or toe or applied to a sty on the eye; black and smelly Ichthyol Ointment brought a cyst or a pimple to a head; and hot tea soothed a stomachache at any time of day or night. Baths infused with Epson salts relaxed aching muscles, and Milk of Magnesia cured not only upset stomachs but also the headaches that were associated with them. Worry and anxiety were eased by the soft touch of my mother's hand over my forehead and brow as I lay weeping on my bed, and no thermometer was as accurate as my mother's lips on my forehead to tell if I had a temperature.

When I was seven years old, someone gave me a toy clarinet. For some reason, I decided to blow the instrument directly into the ear of our pet cocker spaniel Buster while he was sleeping. Not too bright, I admit! When I blasted the sound, Buster jumped up, ramming the clarinet down my throat, causing me to hemorrhage. Instead of calling an ambulance or rushing me off to the hospital, my mother called my father in his dry cleaning store where he was working. She instructed him to bring home a gallon of ice cream. This icy cold remedy stopped the bleeding, and no additional treatment was required. It turned out to be a very pragmatic and effective cure for hemorrhaging from the throat.

Leave it to Rosie!

CAROL'S NAIVETÉ

September 4, 2000 *(journal entry)*

They are smoking marijuana in the back room of the local thrift shop where they receive donations for their organization, and I am appalled. It is the year two thousand, and we have completed three-quarters of the first year of the new millennium. Yet I am shocked that the workers are smoking pot! My moral compass, my point of view, my expectations of behavior by my fellow human beings, my naiveté, my prudishness are stuck in the 1950s and 1960s. I don't use a computer; I have no idea how to "surf" the Internet; I prefer pad and pen to a word processor; and I view electric typewriters and fax machines as new-fangled inventions. I find pornography, foul language, and violent movies offensive. I am not what you would call a modern woman, but rather a woman who has been relatively sheltered, protected, and, for the most part, spared from conflict.

This realization of who I am is rather amazing, considering the fact that I considered myself liberated long before it was in vogue. In 1968, I became the sole breadwinner of our household. With my newly-earned master's degree in hand, I landed a job at my alma mater, The City College of New York, teaching students who were about my age. The births of my three children conveniently coincided with the college closings: Todd was born in the spring of 1969 when the students had shut down the university in protest leading to the policy of Open Admissions; Jeff, at the end of the summer of 1971, three weeks before the start of the fall semester; and Emily during spring break in 1975.

During the early years, while my husband was deeply entrenched in the grueling years of medical school and training, I was blessed with the security and happiness of a loving marriage and the unconditional love and support of my parents. However, I alone bore the responsibilities of working, shopping, cooking, making and keeping doctors' appointments, and taking the children to after-school activities. Paying bills, juggling my private and my professional life, trying to balance my time around three healthy, active children, an overworked and overtired loving husband, and a challenging job provided me with all the female freedom I needed long before I even was aware of the term "women's lib."

Three

Ode to Peggy

April 15, 1990 **(journal entry)**
(handwritten in pencil)

It is Easter Sunday, and I think that Peggy is dying. My physician husband is sure that she is.

A strong, robust, happy woman, Peggy came into my life almost twenty years ago. We have had a close relationship ever since. She has been a second mother to me and a third grandmother to my children. And now she is fading fast.

Peggy was a forty-five-year-old struggling black grandmother who was living in a drug-infested walk-up on 112th Street in Harlem, depending on Medicaid for healthcare and relying on the City to subsidize her rent, while holding down three part-time jobs. Meanwhile, I was a twenty-five-year-old white Jewish young mother who was married to a freshman at New York Medical College, living in a Mitchell-Lama Housing Project in East Harlem and working as a lecturer at City College.

How and why did two so seemingly diametrically opposite human beings find each other and eventually develop such a strong bond of love, friendship, respect, and caring? The reason was a sixteen-month-old baby named Todd.

After spending a year bringing my toddler to wonderfully helpful relatives on the days that I worked, I was thoroughly exhausted. On Mondays, he went to my sister in Teaneck; Wednesdays found him in the care of my mother-in-law in the Bronx; and on Fridays, he spent the day with my parents in Spring Valley. By the time I arrived at my teaching job in New York City, I felt as though I had already put in a full day's work. When the spring semester was over, I decided it was time to find a better situation for Todd's care and my sanity.

I answered "Situations Wanted" ads in the **New York Times***. Two, in particular, stand out in my mind. One woman wanted to know if I had a nice wardrobe for the baby so she could dress him up when she took him to the park. I think she was under the misimpression that East 108th Street was the posh Upper East Side of Manhattan. In fact, it is Spanish Harlem, and my prospective nanny, who would wear starched white uniforms and pictured herself wheeling my baby in a coach-style perambulator, seemed relieved when I told her that she was not the right person for the job.*

I responded to another ad in the **Times***. The person on the other end of the telephone line was essentially non-communicative. Assuming that she felt uncomfortable or was too shy to engage in conversation, I proceeded to describe the job to her. She would have to work the three days a week I taught at City College with the sole responsibility of caring for my sixteen-month-old baby. I rattled on and on about where I lived, what her hours would be, assuring her that no housework would be required. There was still no sign of life on the other end of the phone. In desperation, I finally asked her how much she would charge. The four-word response, "Three dollars an hour" was the first utterance from the woman. After I said that the amount would be all right, she offered me the second and* longest response of the entire conversation: "You mean you'll pay me three dollars an hour!" I told her I would let her know.

It was now August, and the school year was about to begin. I dreaded the thought of dragging Todd around from place to place, loading and unloading his wooden port-o-crib, his favorite toys, bottles, baby food, and all the paraphernalia that a toddler requires. Desperate and frustrated, I called a colleague who had a college student living with her who helped take care of her ten-year-old daughter. I asked her if she knew of another student who might be willing to live with me and watch Todd while I worked. She told me she didn't know about any other students, but her housekeeper had a friend who was between jobs and did not live far from me, just across Fifth Avenue and Central Park on West 112th Street.

The moment she called me back with the phone number, I called Peggy. It was like a breath of fresh air! I was talking to a person who was on my wavelength. She was talkative, friendly, and responsive. We made an appointment to meet later that week. She was the person I had been looking for. She was perfect. She loved children. She exuded kindness and love. She even baked apple pies! She was hired on the spot. And that was how two apparently mismatched women crossed paths.

Well-meaning relatives admonished me about having a stranger help raise my baby. He might become distant, develop psychological problems, form values different from my own. Nothing could have been further from the truth. If anything, Peggy enhanced Todd's, and later Jeffrey's and Emily's lives. She taught them the differences between right and wrong and respect for their fellow man, values that they hold dear to this day. They loved her as much as they loved their own blood-related grandmothers.

In her later years, Peggy's poor health required her to live in a nursing home. During one of his visits to the nursing home, Jeffrey told the nurse he was there to see his grandmother. Together, they scanned the dining room looking for her.

"There she is," Jeffrey shouted, as the nurse looked on with a bemused expression on her face while Jeffrey, with his light brown hair and fair complexion, ran over and embraced his black "grandmother" Peggy.

Through the years, Peggy has been like a mother to me. She has been my friend and confidante, enriching my life as well as the lives of my children. Two days after bringing Emily home from the hospital, I got dressed and came downstairs. She took one look at me and asked, "Where do you think you're going?"

"I'm going to meet Pearl for lunch at Bloomingdale's," I replied.

"No you're not. You're not going anywhere! You just had a baby. Get upstairs right this minute and take a nap!" And like a dutiful daughter, I listened to her.

She related stories of struggle and survival. Peggy was born in Birmingham, Alabama, the third child and only daughter of Charles and Mildred Pope, both of whom were first generation of freed slaves. Her father died working in the coal mines, where he succumbed to black lung disease; and her mother worked all day out in the hot fields of the deep South digging holes for fence-posts, returning home exhausted, where she washed and ironed clothes with so much starch that "they could stand by themselves." Peggy reminisced about walking to school, teased by the other children because she wore her mother's oversized coat which hung down to the ground, but it was the only coat she had so she kept her chin high, knowing that her mother was doing the best she could. I heard heart-wrenching descriptions of jobs that were devoid of human compassion. One job required her to keep the huge white marble dining room floor located in a brownstone mansion on Manhattan's exclusive Upper East Side constantly polished, causing her to drag herself home, hunched over in pain. There were houses where she was not allowed to eat; threats of dismissal for not working on Thanksgiving, crying because her own little girl was home alone on this day of giving thanks; verbal abuses for using Brillo on the silverware or serving the meal to the wrong side of the guest. Yet her spirit was never broken. A devout Baptist, she always kept her faith.

She often recounted happy memories of working for the famous *actress, Angela Lansbury. Whenever she appeared in a play on Broadway, Ms. Lansbury sent her chauffeur to bring Peggy to the performance. Angela's husband showered Peggy with gifts of perfume and trinkets from his many trips abroad. Peggy, who was the same age as Angela, loved working for the movie star. I felt flattered that Peggy chose to stay with me instead of following Angela when she relocated to the West Coast. Even though I never met her, I always felt a secret connection with the famous star because both our lives were touched by Peggy.*

I learned pragmatic solutions to mundane problems. Sayings like "When money changes hands, people change their minds;" or explaining to me that folks who display irrational behavior "ain't wrapped too tight."

And now I am the same age that Peggy was when our paths first crossed, and I think she is dying. Maybe I have written this entry in pencil instead of ink so that the thought of her dying can be eradicated, or that her impending death can be erased and not come to pass.

* * *

seven years later . . . .

MY EULOGY FOR PEGGY POPE
January 4, 1997

I spoke to Peggy last night. I was so happy to see her because Donna, her oldest granddaughter, had just called to tell me that Peggy had died. But Peggy was smiling, riding in the locomotive of a train while trying to reconnect an oxygen tube so that she could breathe easier. It was a wonderful dream. But it was only a dream.

Over the past seven years, Peggy has been a survivor, fighting the ravages of diabetes and high blood pressure, keeping her faith in God and in her love of people and of life itself. An active woman all her life, she bravely adjusted to drastic changes in her circumstances when others would have given up. She came to grips with the amputations of both legs, increased trouble breathing, and confinement to a wheelchair. Despite all this, she was always positive, forever concerned about her friends and family.

I was one of the more fortunate to know her. The fact that our paths crossed at all tells me that our lifelong relationship was meant to be. Twenty-six years ago, I needed someone to care for my baby while I worked. I called a coworker who knew Peggy's good friend, Flo, who told her about Peggy, who called me, and the rest, as they say, is history.

Over the years, our friendship developed into more of a family than merely a work relationship. I was asked to speak here at her funeral, the only non-Baptist, non-black speaker. All of the others are deacons of the church. What an honor! Peggy has been like a second mother to Steve and me, a special grandmother to my children, and a dear friend, confidante, and soulmate.

My daughter Emily told me that the reason she loved Peggy so much was because Peggy always loved her unconditionally. And that was the way Peggy loved everyone close to her. There was never an ulterior motive. There was no questioning. There was just love. Her inspiration; her ability to overcome incredible obstacles, including challenging health problems; her loving ways; her common-sense advice; her belief in God and in people - will be a lasting legacy for all of us.

When Emily came home from work two days ago, she told me she had seen the most beautiful sunset over the Twin Towers. Mesmerized by its magnificence and beauty, Emily viewed the sunset as Peggy transcending her worldly life, looking down on all of us with unquestioning love and inspiration. Peggy will always be with us with her smile warming our hearts and her soul shining down on us.

PART EIGHT

What Would Rosie Say?

One

Author's Note on What Would Rosie Say?

My mother Rosie may not have been in the same league as Benjamin Franklin, Helen Keller, Mahatma Gandhi, or so many others who are remembered for their pearls of wisdom, but she had an innate, uncanny ability to say just the right thing at the right time. Much of what she said was original and uniquely hers, but many of the expressions she used were steeped in history that she adopted as part of her repertoire of sagacious bits of advice. Regardless of their origin, everything that Rosie said was apropos and right on target. When I was able to identify the origin of a particular expression that Rosie used, I referenced it in this chapter. Those of you who speak Yiddish, please accept my apologies if I managed to butcher the phrases that Rosie uttered daily. I have tried to recollect and reconstruct them from memory as best I could.

I hope that this chapter, "What Would Rosie Say?" will give you better insight into Rosie's philosophy on life and provide you with the same enrichment I enjoyed well into middle age. One of the readers of **Rosie (and me)** was so impressed with Rosie's advice that when she was confronted with a serious dilemma, she asked herself, "I wonder, what would Rosie say?" So, Stefani Milan, in addition to your mentoring and support of my writing, thank you for giving me the inspiration and also the title for this chapter, "What Would Rosie Say?"

Two

What Rosie Said

Two minds with a single thought

"Two souls with but a single thought.   Two hearts that beat as one!"

John Keats

Rosie used this expression when we both had the same idea or shared the same viewpoint on a particular matter.

* * *

Make haste slowly

In her 8th-grade autograph album, Rosie cited this as her favorite motto. It suggests that we should do things both efficiently and carefully but not jeopardize quality just because we want to get something done quickly. Caesar Augustus is said to have first adopted the motto: *Festina Lente - Make haste slowly*. He had gold coins printed with a crab and a butterfly to symbolize the idea. Over the centuries, many other images have been created to remind us of the adage, telling us to go slow to go fast, such as a hare in a snail shell or a dolphin entwined around an anchor.

* * *

No one sees their own hunch

"The camel can't see its own hump." - Greek proverb

We easily criticize and point out other people's faults and weaknesses, but we often fail to see those very same shortcomings in ourselves.

* * *

Patience is a virtue

In *The Canterbury Tales*, Geoffrey Chaucer calls patience a high virtue. It is a very good trait to be patient, going so far as to call it a virtue. But if we young children were misbehaving, after altruistically saying that patience is a virtue, Rosie would mumble under her breath, "But who wants to be virtuous!"

* * *

As I live and breathe

This expression dates back to the mid-1600s and is generally used to emphasize the truth of a statement or the surprise one experiences at an unexpected occurrence. Rosie exclaimed this sentiment whenever she received a phone call out of the blue from someone she hadn't heard from in a long time or if she unexpectedly encountered a person she knew.

* * *

A fair exchange is no robbery

A deal should benefit both parties equally, and neither party should feel that the other person is getting the better deal. The proverbial saying "a fair exchange is no robbery" is found as early as 1546 in a comprehensive collection of English proverbs by John Heywood.

* * *

God helps those who help themselves

The saying is usually attributed to Ben Franklin, quoted in **Poor Richard's Almanack** in 1757. Some people believe that the phrase actually originated in ancient Greece as "the gods help those who help themselves."

Rosie encouraged all of us to fend for ourselves and advised us not to rely on others for our success. She didn't want her children to be needy or beholden to anyone. An example of this was her insistence that I take secretarial classes even though I was on the academic track at Spring Valley High School. I remember our meeting with Mr. Sugarman, the principal of the high school, who argued that since I was college-bound, I should not take shorthand and typing. But Rosie was equally adamant that she would not allow her daughter to be without the necessary skills to earn a living if, as had happened to her, college did not pan out. Rosie won the argument, and some of my fondest memories were interacting with the students in those secretarial classes, so different from my friends who were on the academic track.

* * *

Hindsight is 20-20

"Most people's hindsight is 20-20" was attributed to humorist Richard Armour in 1949. Rosie was correct when she pointed out that we see things so clearly in retrospect!

* * *

Then there were excellent words of marital advice that were uniquely Rosie's.

Never go to bed angry.
Always say "I love you" to your spouse before going to sleep.
Never argue in front of your children.

* * *

She often encouraged her children, and later, her grandchildren, in their endeavors by saying, "I've **got my money on you.**"

If one of her children was suffering from physical discomfort or emotional turmoil, she selflessly commiserated (in Yiddish), **Bessa bi mir.** - "It should happen to me instead."

She was tenaciously protective of her children and was adamant when she declared, *"Hurt me but not my child."*

And she was of the strong belief that *"If you can't take it, don't dish it out."* This admonition always was uttered when, as children often do, we would tease one another unmercifully, often resulting in someone crying or getting angry.

In this vein, she also would say (in Yiddish): *"Mach nicht kein khokhmes"* reminding us that too much fooling around or teasing one another invariably results in someone getting upset. (Note: I never asked my mother about the origin of this phrase and have since learned that *Khokhmes* literally means *wisdom.* I am assuming she meant not to be a smart aleck.)

* * *

With regard to her declining physical condition that prevented her from doing the things she loved to do, she was of good humor when she said, *"The mind is willing, but the body isn't able."*

When asked how she was doing, we could expect her reply to be, "I'm *in good shape for the shape I'm in!"*

She laughed when she reminded me that my uncle Hymie, who lived well into his nineties, would say, *"If I knew I would live this long, I would have taken better care of myself!"*

And when I told her she was eating something really healthy, she responded with a smile, *"If I eat this for a hundred years, I'll live long."*

But if she was tempted to eat something she knew was not good for her, like candy or ice cream, she would admit, *"One is too much. One hundred is not enough.".* . . so don't even take that first bite!

* * *

Even though she was blind and confined to her wheelchair, she tried desperately to maintain her independence, never demanding nor burdensome, but when she needed help, she reluctantly asked, *"If it wouldn't be too much trouble, darling, would you mind getting me (e.g.) a glass of water?"*

Her entreaty to God is one of my favorite expressions:

Gut shrek mir, but shtrof mir nischt.
(God frighten me, but don't punish me.)

As I mentioned in an earlier chapter, these words echoed in my mind while my husband was undergoing major surgery for prostate cancer. Who could know that her words would resonate with me eight years after she died. But all of Rosie's words of wisdom are timeless and stay with me each and every day.

So when Steve was diagnosed with cancer, I realized that God had *shreked* (frightened) us but hoped He would not *shtrof* (punish) us, too. Sitting in the Quiet Room at Fox Chase Cancer Center on what would have been my father's 99th birthday, I concentrated on my mother's reassuring smile, reflecting on the comfort she had always given me.

I heard her voice in my head, "Don't worry, *ketzila* (Yiddish - "little kitten"). He will be okay." I clung to her words as I sat in the room filled with bibles of every religion set aside for family members to meditate while their loved ones were facing the biggest medical challenge of their lives. And just as her words had reassured me so many times in the past, everything turned out okay.

It is a phrase I use often, always praying for a good outcome. When I had chest pain, jaw pain, sweating, and shortness of breath, I was lucky. Instead of the heart attack I feared, it turned out to be a bad case of indigestion. Once again, I thought to myself with relief that God had frightened me, but He didn't punish me.

Although they had their differences, Rosie agreed wholeheartedly with my father's oldest sister, my aunt Sarah, when she said, *"If you try to please everyone, you end up pleasing no one, especially not yourself."*

* * *

When your children are young, they may make a mess when they try to help; they spill their milk; they get crumbs all over the floor; they flood the kitchen when they wash the dishes; they scratch the fender when they parallel park. When they are older, they can disappoint you in ways that break your heart. Some children hang out with the wrong friends, get hooked on drugs, contract terrible diseases, or find themselves in financial difficulty. Others might ignore you or, worse, merely tolerate you. "Just remember," Rosie would say, *"when they're little, they step on your toes. When they're big, they step on your heart."* The toes or the heart? Which is better to be stepped upon? For me, the choice is clear.

* * *

The single most important person in Rosie's life was her husband. If I invited her to dinner, the response was, "Let me ask Daddy." Once, she created an uproar when she declined an invitation to a family birthday party so her *Shimshee* wouldn't miss his bowling night. Rosie did not care about any repercussions. Simon came first. She defended him to the end. There was no question. She often drilled into me her firm belief that *"the most important person in your life is your mate. Then come your children. And after that, your parents."*

I have emulated this in my own marriage of over fifty years, and I have passed the advice onto my married children. Rosie was right, as usual. When all is said and done, it is your mate who is always there, both physically and emotionally, when you are in need or when you are not. He is the one I can always count on, the stalwart in my corner, the pillar of my existence.

* * *

Even though my mother was a chain smoker, I never confessed to her that I smoked; and I was never much of a drinker. Her admonition, *"If you smoke, smoke your own. If you drink, drink your own"* was clearly stated to me anytime I was about to find myself in a situation where people would be drinking and smoking. She warned me that someone might spike my drink or give me a cigarette that contained something other than tobacco. I would listen patiently, smiling to myself, but heed her warning nonetheless.

* * *

Rosie empathized and related to everyone, young and old alike, never dismissing a person's concerns simply because of their age. She maintained that *"the problems of a two-year-old are just as serious to him as the problems of a fifteen-year-old, a forty-year-old, a sixty-year-old, or an eighty-year-old are to them."* So the angst that a toddler feels when losing his security blanket is just as serious to him as the teenager losing her boyfriend, the forty-year-old losing his job, the sixty-year-old losing his retirement money, or the eighty-year-old losing her independence.

Rosie rarely made what she referred to as "a big *tsimmes* (fuss)" about things. If something was troubling me and I didn't know the solution, she would often say, "*Ketzila*, **zog dos nischt**. *Ketzila, don't worry. . .so fast my arthritis should heal up.*" She put things in the order of their priority, placing everything in its proper perspective. Nothing was a big deal. She never belittled anyone else's problems, and she invariably put a positive spin on seemingly negative situations. If the roof leaked or if a tree fell on the fence, she minimized my over-reaction, "Carola," she would say, "It's *only money; and with money you get honey.*" When I expressed my concern that a particular plan I had was not going to come to fruition, she often said, "*Yeah, yeah. Nischt, nischt.*" If it happens, fine. If not, well that's okay, too. And if I got upset over what someone said or did, she would uncharacteristically blurt out, "*Carola. It's a bunch of shit!*"

* * *

A child of the Great Depression, Rosie was never a fan of old things. Brand-new, never-before-used items meant more to her than antiques. Used furniture didn't have the allure for her that it did for me. So when I proudly showed off my new antique dining room table, pointing out its nicks and scratches and antique patina, Rosie was not impressed. She exclaimed, "*I burnt better!*" or a slightly different take on the same theme, "*I threw out better!*"

***

Okay. I admit it. I was always an overachiever, and I never felt satisfied that I had studied enough, memorized enough, or fully processed all of the information I needed to know before an exam. At dinner, after having studied continually for weeks, I would rush through my meal, explaining to my mother that I had to study some more for an upcoming test. She reminded me that I had already devoted an inordinate amount of time studying. "Just go to sleep," she would advise. *"Remember, a well-rested body is a well-rested mind."* Sometimes, she would gratuitously add, *"Only the smart kids are nervous about a test. The dummies never worry!"*

In retrospect, I realize that what she said was absolutely true. When I stubbornly stayed up most of the night studying, pulling an all-nighter, I tended to do worse on a test than those times I heeded her advice and got a good night's sleep.

At times like these, she would also assure me, *"A hundred years from now, nobody will know the difference!"*

Rosie should have been a child psychologist. She missed her calling!

***

And then there are the two sayings that were carry-overs from Rosie's father. She often quoted him as saying: "It's *better to be the smartest of the dumbest than the dumbest of the smartest."* In other words, it's better to be a big fish in a small pond than a small fish in a big pond.

I invariably got stumped when she tested our math skills and asked: *"If a herring and a half cost a penny and a half, how much do six herrings cost?"* No wonder I didn't major in math!

* * *

Charity begins at home

Rosie was a firm believer that family came first. She ferociously protected her children and was unwavering in her love and support of her husband. This saying, though, is not a Rosie original.

The notion that a man's family should be his foremost concern is mentioned in 1 Timothy 5:8, **King James Bible**, 1611: "But if any provide not for his owne, and specially for those of his owne house, he hath denied the faith, and is worse than an infidel."

John Wyclif expressed the same idea as early as 1382 in **Of Prelates**, reprinted in 1880: "Charite schuld bigyne at hem-self."

It appears in the English satirist John Marston's play **Histrio-Mastix**, published in 1610: "True charity beginneth first at home."

Sir Thomas Browne was the first to put the expression into print in the form we now use, in **Religio Medici**, 1642: "Charity begins at home, is the voice of the world."

* * *

You catch more flies with honey than with vinegar

This proverb is said to have originated in 1666 and is found in Giovani Torriano's **A Common Place of Italian Proverbs and Proverbial Phrases**: "Honey gets more flyes to it, than doth vinegar." *(Italian: Il mile catta piu mosche, che non fa l'aceto)*.

Eighty years later, Benjamin Franklin included it in his 1744 publication of **Poor Richard's Almanack**: "Tart words make no friends: a spoonful of honey will catch more flies than a gallon of vinegar."

In her own quiet, unassuming way, Rosie managed to charm people without being obnoxious. She never sounded like a snake-oil salesman, a carnival barker, or a conniver. She was just herself. She was convinced that people are more inclined to help you if you are polite, ingratiating, and kind to them, rather than hostile, demanding, bitter, or nasty. And she practiced what she preached!

At the age of fifty-three, she learned how to drive, and after knocking down the cones that were supposed to guide her in the parallel parking segment of her driver's test, she charmed the officer who gave her the test, promising that she would **never** parallel park, and he passed her! "See, Rosie, it's true," she said to herself. "You **do** catch more flies with honey than with vinegar!"

* * *

Give your children roots and wings

After her three children were out on their own, I never once heard Rosie complain that she was now an empty-nester. I don't think the thought ever entered her mind. She once told me that there were two things parents must give their children: roots and wings. The phrase has been around for centuries and has been attributed to various sources. One is Jonas Salk, who developed one of the first successful polio vaccines. He said that good parents give their children roots and wings - roots to know where home is and wings to fly away and exercise what they have been taught. The German writer and statesman, Johann Wolfgang von Goethe alluded to it in the 18th century; it is said to be a Chinese proverb; and the Dalai Lama has also been credited with the saying.

But I learned it from Rosie!

* * *

Want what you have

"You shall not covet your neighbor's house; you shall not covet your neighbor's wife, or his male servant, or his female servant, or his ox, or his donkey, or anything that is your neighbor's" (The 10th Commandment) Exodus 20:17

I cannot remember a time when Rosie envied someone else's good fortune or success. She was truly happy in her own skin and was a strong believer that you should want what you have. If you follow this advice, you can never be unhappy because you will not desire anything more than what you already have. We were taught to value the blessings that we had and not look for *goldena glicken*. (Yiddish - dreams that are impossible to attain).

Glancing toward the sign on her wall with the old Persian proverb, *"I cried because I had no shoes until I met a man who had no feet,"* she would say to me, "Don't forget, *Ketzila*, you may think that others have it better than you, but **you never know** *vous titzik by yenem"* (Yiddish - You never know what's really happening behind the scenes with other people). The lovey-dovey Hollywood couple will be on the cover of *People* magazine next week announcing their divorce. The seemingly wealthy man who lives next door is on food stamps, and the vivacious woman who looks so healthy is battling stage 4 lymphoma."

Rosie often said, *"Everyone has their own cross to bear, and if people put their problems in the middle of a room and saw the sufferings of others, they would be happy to take their own problems back."*

* * *

A penny saved is a penny earned
Benjamin Franklin
Poor Richard's Almanack, 1732

Turning sixteen in 1929, Rosie was directly affected by the Great Depression. It hit everyone hard, including her own wealthy family; and Rosie's dreams and aspirations of going to college to become a schoolteacher were dashed. The Depression taught her the importance of saving money, and she learned from experience that it is easier to save the money you already have than it is to earn more. She tried to teach us not to squander money on nonsensical, unimportant things. If I wanted to buy a new dress, she would say, "What do you need another *shmata* (Yiddish - rag) for? You already have plenty of *shmatas* in your closet!" If I announced that I was going to buy something that I clearly did not need, she would tell me, "You need it like a *lochen kop*." (Yiddish - like a hole in the head). She totally disapproved of buying anything on credit, and she didn't even get a credit card until she was in her eighties when she got an offer for one with no annual fee. She was so firm in her convictions not to ever buy anything until you had the cash to pay for it that when I first got married and decided to take out a $1,500 loan to buy furniture, I never told my mother for fear that she would reprimand me for not taking her sound advice. She once told me how she kept eyeing a mirror at Wanamaker's, the department store in New York City that was located at 770 Broadway between 8th and 9th Streets, about ten blocks from her apartment. After carefully saving up the forty dollars that the mirror cost, she was finally able to pay for it in cash. She valued this possession more than if she had waved a credit card at the salesperson and acquired the mirror without any sacrifice. I have that mirror hanging prominently in my home and am reminded of this story every time I look at it.

* * *

Waste not, want not

(originally, "Willful waste makes woeful want" - from *The Paradise of Dainty Devices* [1576] by Richard Edwardes, a distinguished lyricist and playwright who was rumored to be an illegitimate son of Henry VIII.)

Many of Rosie's expressions revolved around her being careful with money. In no way was she stingy, but she was also very thrifty. She believed that wise use of your money would keep you from going broke. Her theory was that if you do not waste your resources, you will never be in need.

* * *

Ask me no questions. I'll tell you no lies

I can think of no one who was more tuned in to the feelings of others than Rosie. In the the Torah portion *Parsha Vayechi*, Joseph withholds the truth from Jacob about how his brothers had sold him into slavery. He wants to spare his father the pain he would feel if he learned that Jacob's other sons had committed such a heinous act against Jacob's favorite son Joseph. Rosie, too, tried very hard not to hurt the feelings of others, so if someone were to ask her a question the answer to which might be unpleasant or unsettling, Rosie found herself in the difficult situation of being forced to either evade the question altogether or outright lie. She did not suffer liars and drilled into us that for her, **"There's one thing I hate and that's a liar and a cheat."** So rather than lying to someone where telling the truth might be hurtful, she chose to avoid answering the question altogether. That is why she said, "Ask me no questions. I'll tell you no lies."

***

You can't put an old head on young shoulders

The American writer, Horatio Alger was famous for his books

depicting the "rags-to-riches" stories of young boys in New York during the mid-nineteenth century. *"You can't put an old head on young shoulders"* appeared in his book, *The Young Outlaw* (1875). Rosie quoted this phrase to me if I was disappointed with the behavior of one of my children or surprised when I heard about a bad decision made by a young person. The meaning is pertinent in that it implies that a young person cannot be expected to have or display the wisdom and sound judgment that we come to expect from someone who is older and more experienced. In the same vein, my father reassured me whenever I realized I had made a poor decision after not heeding his advice that it was not that he was smarter than I, only that he had been around longer and had more experience.

* * *

Every crooked pot has a crooked cover

"So every beast finds a mate, and from the same fact comes the proverb, 'There is no pot, however ugly, that does not one day find a cover.'"

Honore de Balzac (1799-1850)
The Maid of Thilouse

Everybody has someone out there who is just right for him. It doesn't matter what you look like, what your political views are, or how complicated your personality is, there is someone who is on your wavelength and will be perfectly compatible with you.

When Rosie said, *"Every crooked pot has a crooked cover,"* she was expressing her belief that she valued the worth of others regardless of their idiosyncrasies. Even when someone's beliefs, personality, or physical attributes were vastly different from her own, she respected that person for his convictions. Clearly, we all don't see the world in the same way nor do we view everyone in the same light. If she disagreed with someone, rather than become angry or argumentative, Rosie would smile with an understanding look on her face and sigh, *"To each his own."*

* * *

Give people the benefit of the doubt

Rosie strongly believed that we should give people the benefit of the doubt, and she made every effort to overlook what someone did or said that angered her or made her feel bad. So, for instance, if someone cuts you off while driving, rather than experience road rage, it is better to think that perhaps the driver is rushing to the hospital with a sick child or going to visit his dying mother.

Nowadays, it seems that no one wants to give anyone else the benefit of the doubt. So many people are ready to attack others for their thoughts, actions, and ideas, never even trying to see things from their point of view. The world would be such a better place if we all listened to Rosie!

* * *

Self-praise stinks!

Rosie disliked braggarts and people who were overly impressed with themselves. She had a wonderful balance of complimenting her children on their achievements without over-inflating their egos. Whenever I would find myself patting myself on the back for something I had achieved, Rosie would gently say "S.P.S." reminding me that self-praise stinks!

Rosie gave unconditional love but refused to give unconditional, undeserved praise. She never failed to compliment us for our accomplishments, but neither would she automatically tell us how great we were. Unlike many parents today, as well as Little League coaches who give a trophy to everyone, winners and losers alike, she never gave us a false sense of accomplishment when we fell short of her expectations.

She told us, *"When God gave out brains, you were at the front of the line,"* as our chests swelled with pride, *"but then God said, 'A...BOUT face'."* A humble person by nature, she was careful to keep our egos in check, so when we became full of ourselves because Rosie implied that we were at the front of the line, she made sure our egos didn't get too big by telling us what God said next!

* * *

Give credit where credit is due

Even if Rosie disagreed with someone or was not especially fond of them, she insisted upon giving credit where credit was due. Acknowledging that someone has done something meritorious does not mean that you have to like him or agree with him all the time, but you should not hesitate to recognize that what that person did was praiseworthy.

It reminds me of the current political situation where those who hate former President Trump with such vitriol refuse to acknowledge his part in Operation Warped Speed, by which he accelerated the development of a COVID-19 vaccine. Another one of his accomplishments was the Abraham Accord. On August 13, 2020,

Israel and the United Arab Emirates (UAE) signed an agreement mediated by President Trump, bringing together centuries-long enemies in the Middle East. Under the deal, Israel and the UAE established full diplomatic relations, making the UAE the third Arab state, besides Egypt and Jordan, to fully recognize Israel. This monumental accomplishment was praised by many who thought that President Trump's efforts in affecting such an accord merited a Nobel Peace Prize. His adversaries, however, refused to acknowledge the importance of the historic agreement and could not even bring themselves around to give credit where credit was due.

These naysayers should take heed of Rosie's advice that you don't have to love someone in order to recognize their achievements.

* * *

Here's an expression that my sister Pearl suggested I leave out, but Rosie said it so often that I could not resist including it. Despite the painful rheumatoid arthritis that plagued her for her entire adult life, Rosie never failed to prepare home-cooked meals. The discomfort she felt could not have made the process easy. It was not uncommon for us little kids to pester her unyieldingly, inquiring about what we were having for dinner. With a twinkle in her eye and a smile upon her lips, she would look at us and exclaim, "*Drek mit leber!*" (Yiddish - "Shit with liver!") I never heard her using that phrase in any other context, but it is a well-known Yiddish phrase often used to mean "less than nothing."

* * *

No one is born a minute before his time nor dies a minute after his time

Rosie was a fatalist. She was a strong believer that everything happens for a reason, and nothing is left to chance. According to Jewish law, the sacred time between Rosh Hashanah and Yom Kippur is the time when one's fate is determined for the entire coming year. Jews believe that "on Rosh Hashanah it is written, and on Yom Kippur it is sealed." It is said that at the close of Yom Kippur, the Book of Life is closed, sealing our fate for the year ahead. As a person brought up steeped in the tenets of Judaism, Rosie truly believed that the moment we are born and the exact moment that we die are pre-determined.

* * *

The mensch tracht, and Gut lacht!
(People make plans, and God laughs!)

How many times have we made elaborate plans only to have them dashed because of some unexpected occurrence? It has happened to all of us. Rosie experienced this first-hand when she was all set to go to Hunter College ready to embark on the path to become a schoolteacher when the Depression hit, and she was forced to go to work instead. We may look forward to going on the vacation of a lifetime only to be met with the disappointment of an unexpected illness or family emergency. To this day, I still recall my disappointment as a young child when I was eagerly planning to go to the movies but couldn't because of some unforeseen hurdle. We once made elaborate plans to go fishing in Long Island Sound with our infant son when he suddenly came down with a stomach virus, and we couldn't go. And how can any of us ever forget all of the plans so many people made that were cancelled because of the COVID-19 pandemic? Whether our plans are monumental or mundane, they are often interrupted by some outside force beyond our control. When this occurs, the Yiddish saying, *"The mensch tracht, and Gut lacht!"* rings true each and every time.

Fardrey bist in kop and dinka is mein kop
(You're crazy in the head and you think I'm the one who's crazy!)

The millennials call it "gaslighting." The word keeps popping up lately, especially among political opponents, each thinking that the other side is crazy. Gaslighting is a form of psychological abuse where a person or group makes others question their sanity, perception of reality, or memories. The term originated in the 1930s stage play called **Gaslight**, wherein a husband tries to convince his wife that she is insane by manipulating her environment in subtle ways.

But Rosie's way of expressing the same sentiment in Yiddish was so much more colorful and musical. I can remember her saying in Yiddish, *"Fardrey bist in kop* and *dinka is mein kop."* [loose translation] - *"You're crazy in the head and you think I'm the one who's crazy!"*

* * *

Leap and a net will appear
John Burroughs
(nineteenth century author and naturalist)

I never actually heard Rosie use this phrase, but I have taken the liberty to include it anyway because in her eighth-grade autograph album, she referred to John Burroughs (1877-1921) as her favorite hero. She followed his advice, always expecting a net to appear whenever she took that proverbial leap. She gave up her prosperous existence living with her wealthy parents to marry my penniless father, and she relinquished her comfortable familiar New York City lifestyle to start all over in a run-down abandoned rooming house in the boonies.

This leap of faith is described in detail in **Rosie (and me) - a memoir**, page 25:

Spring Valley, New York

They give up everything in New York City, and when he expresses any doubt in their decision, Rosie reminds my father that in 1927, she wrote in her autograph album that her favorite hero was the naturalist, John Burroughs, who said: "Leap and a net will appear." So they take a leap of faith, and in 1955, they sell their cleaning store in New York City and buy a dilapidated old rooming house in Spring Valley. Rosie helps my father renovate the place, clinging to the memory of her more energetic days when enthusiasm was all that was necessary to keep her going, when she was not encumbered by the pain and limitations of her diseased body. She paints a large sign ANDERMAN'S BUNGALOWS and helps to transform the uninhabitable rooms into comfortable summer apartments to bring in an income. My father, the maverick who stole my mother's heart so many years before, sold Mack Quality Cleaners, his cleaning store on the corner of Fourteenth Street and Seventh Avenue - his only means of support - and moved his entire family to the old rooming house on six acres in Spring Valley that he purchased with his life's savings of sixteen thousand dollars. In our 1954 Kaiser sedan, we follow the rickety moving truck, without a name, that is overflowing with all our worldly belongings. I spot our twelve-inch black-and-white television set, hoping that our prized possession would not fall out of the truck and break during the journey. It could have been a scene from the Beverly Hillbillies *that would air decades later.*

She relinquishes city life with no regrets and proudly slips into her new role as country wife, marveling, "Who would have guessed that Rosie would be married to a city boy turned country squire." Together they oversee their six-acre "estate," one acre of which is dotted with the remaining trees of a long-forgotten apple orchard from which we salvage the partially rotten apples that have fallen from the neglected trees. Most of the apples are inedible, but Rosie manages to cut away the worm holes and soft spots and then cook them into a delicious applesauce using the same vintage Foley mill she uses to make soup from my father's tomato crop.

Together, they design their version of a chicken coop, using wire to surround the abandoned outhouse with the crescent moon cut-out on top that is still standing on the property. We gather enough eggs so "eggs" is no longer added to the grocery list. When we aren't gathering eggs, Rosie commands us to "Go pick some rocks" to keep us occupied during her afternoon naps. She says it in the same intonation and syntax as if she is telling us to "Go pick some flowers" or "Go pick some berries!" We take this job very seriously because it is not merely an exercise in futility to keep us busy. My father uses the small rocks to reinforce the cement he mixes in his miniature cement mixer and then pours to lay a sidewalk or build a porch.

With great anticipation, she opens a small dress shop that she proudly names Anderman Apparel, joining King Kotten and Betty's Corset Shop on Main Street, where she painstakingly and painfully wraps the thirty-nine-cent neckerchief and fifty-nine-cent kerchief in a box with colorful paper and ribbons that she curls using the edge of a pair of scissors. I meet her there after school and help as much as an eleven-year-old can. The store fails - the most expensive item is a dress for $6.98; and my parents put all of their efforts into converting the rooming house into small apartments to be rented on a weekly basis to transients who are newly divorced, alcoholics, or just down on their luck.

She enrolls in the local community college and registers for English and psychology classes, where she wows her professors and young classmates with her insights on family and love. The psychology professor gives her an A-plus on her essay describing the different kinds of love: the romantic love for a spouse, the nurturing love for a child, and the reverent love for a parent. He marvels that his introductory course is the first class in psychology she has ever taken and compliments her on her enormous insight, stating that her explanation of human nature rivals explanations given in most textbooks. At fifty-three, she learns how to drive. She shops for groceries and exercises at Jack LaLanne, always driving home on the exact same route so that my father can find her in case she doesn't make it home.

* * *

On paper, everything looks easy

Whether it is writing a book, editing a film, buying or selling a house, going on a diet, eating properly, or starting a business, it always looks easy on paper. From her experience, Rosie realized that a concept is easy to come by, but the execution of that idea is another story altogether. Once you get down to the nitty-gritty of the task, it is not quite as simple as it looked on paper!

* * *

That's my story, and I'm stuck with it

Although this was one of my father's favorite sayings, Rosie adopted it as well. It was not until recently that I learned that the proper saying is, "That's my story, and I'm sticking with it." This invokes a totally different connotation. My father's version is more pessimistic. My guess is that Rosie would have preferred the more optimistic way of saying it.

* * *

And this, too, shall pass

When the COVID-19 pandemic hit in the winter of 2020, I could not help thinking of what Rosie used to say if she or someone she knew was going through a difficult time. She would assure me, "And this, too, shall pass." She lived through the Spanish Flu pandemic of 1918. She survived the Great Depression. She refused to throw in the towel when faced with misfortune, including the death of her soulmate just short of their golden wedding anniversary. Rosie always managed to adjust, realizing that with time, you can get used to anything.

* * *

Rosie never allowed anything to shock or catch her off guard, and she often used the saying:

Az mo leit, derleit me alas
(If you live long enough, you will live to see everything)

PART NINE

The Dichotomy
of 2020

*A Year of Blurred Vision
and Uncertainty*

One

The Pandemic of 2020

In February of 2020, I cancelled our plans to go to Hawaii because of the emergence of the newly-identified COVID-19 virus. I would be remiss if I didn't devote part of this memoir to the ensuing pandemic caused by this deadly virus. Like those who were alive during the Spanish Flu of 1918, we are living through history with our own 2020 pandemic. It will be invaluable for our progeny to read this contemporaneous commentary about a pandemic whose impact on our society, economy, health, and future will only become clear in retrospect.

At first, the entire coronavirus situation was downplayed by the authorities. Dr. Anthony Fauci, director of the National Institutes of Health and lead doctor on President Trump's Coronavirus Task Force, revered by some and reviled by others, told us that he agreed with the director of the World Health Organization that the virus originated in a wet market in Wuhan, China, where it was transmitted by an infected bat and that there was nothing to worry about because it could not spread from human to human. He also assured us that wearing masks was unnecessary. Heeding Dr. Fauci's advice, people went out, mingled with others, and attended birthday parties, weddings, and funerals without taking sufficient precautions. Subsequently, the number of cases began to skyrocket. People were put on ventilators. The President shut down the economy for fifteen days to flatten the curve of the high number of cases that was spiking at an unprecedented velocity. Schools were closed. Church services were cancelled. Fitness centers were shut down. Weddings were postponed. "Zoom" became a household word and emerged as the newest online platform for people to meet with coworkers, friends, and family.

Initially, it seemed like a blessing in disguise. It would be a time when we could tap into our creative selves and accomplish tasks and chores that we did not have time for before. In fact, I posted this on Facebook on March 20, 2020:

During this time of uncertainty, I find strength in my mother's determination and optimism when she was faced with strife and adversity. It was then that Rosie would say, "And this, too, shall pass!" Take heed, and make the most of this time, for when it is over, we will, once again, be too busy to do those things that have long been placed on the back burner.

We should try to use this time of isolation wisely. Shakespeare wrote **Romeo and Juliet**, **King Lear**, *and* **Macbeth** *during the two months he was in isolation during the Black Death of 1593; and Isaac Newton completed* **The Theory of Gravity and Calculus** *during the bubonic "Great Plague" of 1665–1666.*

* * *

Three journal entries during the previous week reflected my reaction to the pandemic:

March 12, 2020

I am feeling an amazing sense of calm while our entire population grapples with the panic that has erupted as a result of the rapid spread of the coronavirus. Schools, movie theaters, libraries, towns, and even entire countries are in complete lockdown. President Trump has banned not only those travelers from China and Iran (the countries most affected by the virus) but now, all of Europe as well. The threat is real. And yet, I am feeling a sense of calm the likes of which I have never felt before!

* * *

March 17, 2020

The veil has lifted, and the full impact of the global consequences of the pandemic has been unleashed. All schools, gyms, restaurants, and bars in New Jersey and New York have been closed. The President has recommended a 15-day self-quarantine period for everyone, and the elderly are advised to stay at home.

Despite the gloom and doom of many, I am still oddly calm in the midst of this unfolding crisis, which, if we listen to first-hand accounts of people in Spain and Italy, the worst is yet to come. Perhaps I do not fully comprehend the gravity of the situation. I am reminded of a quote in the poem, **Ode on a Distant Prospect of Eton College** *by Thomas Gray (1742), "Where ignorance is bliss, 'tis folly to be wise":*

"To each his sufferings: all are men,
Condemn'd alike to a groan,
The tender for another's pain;
Th' unfeeling for his own.
Yet ah! why should they know their fate?
Since sorrow never comes too late,
And happiness too swiftly flies.
Thought would destroy their paradise.
No more; where ignorance is bliss,
'Tis folly to be wise."

What is it about this impending doom that has drawn me to the great writers of centuries ago? Perhaps it makes me realize that the human condition has not changed very much, and responses to our inevitable fate remain eerily similar.

"I have lived long enough. My way of life
Is fall'n into the sere, the yellow leaf,
And that which should accompany old age,
As honor, love, obedience, troops of friends,
I must not look to have. . ."

Shakespeare **Macbeth**

. . . and finally

"Tomorrow, and tomorrow, and tomorrow,
Creeps in this petty pace from day to day,
To the last syllable of recorded time;
And all our yesterdays have lighted fools
The way to dusty death. Out, out, brief candle!
Life's but a walking shadow, a poor player,
That struts and frets his hour upon the stage,

And then is heard no more. It is a tale
Told by an idiot, full of sound and fury,
Signifying nothing."

Shakespeare Macbeth

* * *

March 18, 2020

My niece, Elissa, posted on Facebook, "WE'RE DOOMED!" The world-wide pandemic has crippled our society; and mathematicians who are weighing in on the exponential acceleration of cases of coronavirus have predicted that the disease has the potential of killing millions of people.

The situation is surreal. How is it possible that mankind, so advanced, is now in such a fragile, difficult fight for its survival? During our walk a few days ago, I told Steve that I can imagine that a few million years from now, researchers will look back and wonder what destroyed the most advanced society ever to inhabit our planet. It will be similar to our conjecture about the extinction of the dinosaurs sixty-six million years ago. The dinosaurs had roamed our planet for 165 million years, and it is now believed that their demise was the result of a massive comet or asteroid 10 to 15 km (6 to 9 mi) wide which devastated the global environment. By comparison, humans and their ancestors have occupied the planet for a mere six million years; so it is not unfathomable for a species to be wiped out completely by a force of nature.

Coronavirus has monopolized the news 24/7. In ancient Greece, Draconian laws were noteworthy for their extreme harshness. They were said to be written in blood, rather than ink, and death was prescribed for almost all criminal offenses. Nowadays, we find many governors of states using their power to arbitrarily close schools, gyms, churches, and stores and imprisoning those who do not follow their own proscribed draconian laws of vaccine and mask mandates.

Our country is the most divided it has been since the Civil War. Vitriol pervades the Internet, and liberals and conservatives try to outdo each other on how hateful their Facebook posts can be. Conservatives call liberals "snowflakes" suffering from Trump derangement syndrome, while liberals refer to conservatives as racists, Nazis, and white supremacists. The hatred is palpable and ubiquitous. It is present everywhere you turn. It is impossible to avoid.

In a conversation I had with my granddaughter, Aviva, we surmised that perhaps God got tired of our constant fighting with each other and decided to give us a time-out, a time to reflect, a time to try to see the other side, a time to make at least some attempt to come together. I recall my mother's reaction when we cried over nonsense or fought over trivial things and she would give us a smack on the rear and say, "Now I'll give you something to cry about!"

* * *

The following journal entries were written during the height of the pandemic between March and August of 2020:

March 20, 2020

The world is on hold. God has pressed the "pause" button and given us all a time-out. Did we misbehave, fight too much with each other, fail to be appreciative, let politics obscure our common sense, refuse to see the good in our fellow man, or all of the above? The country has reacted to this pandemic in many different ways. There are the naysayers who think that the virus is bogus, the avid doomsday pessimists who feel the world is coming to an end, the Trump haters with their vitriolic Facebook posts, the equally abhorrent Trump supporters, the conspiracy theorists, and the skeptics. God help us if we do not come together as a country!

March 27, 2020

Only ten days into the quarantine, and I find the pervasive news covering the coronavirus pandemic is starting to wear me down. The reports of the number of people dying from the virus remind me of the headlines during the Vietnam War. Each morning, the news consisted of how many body bags were brought back to the United States, indicating the number of young men that had been killed in Vietnam since the previous day. I find myself on edge. The eery sense of calm that I possessed has passed, and the constant infiltration of the facts, and sometimes fiction, of the virus has become so overwhelming that I realize I must take a break from it all.

* * *

March 31, 2020

The pandemic has forced us into a new way of life. Everyone is mandated to be self-quarantined, and businesses and schools are closed. The conspiracy theorists liken it to a new world order and warn us that it is only a matter of time before the government takes over completely. The news is so filled with doom and gloom that I have stopped watching the news on television, and I turn off the radio if the broadcasts become too negative or political. The rapidity with which everything has been shut down is mind-boggling, and I can see how my niece, Elissa, is convinced that this is all a ploy by the government to get the people ("sheeple" - as she calls them) to do whatever it demands.

* * *

April 12, 2020

The coronavirus pandemic and accompanying self-isolation have people reacting in so many different ways. It is George Orwell's book, *1984*, playing out in real time. My liberal relatives who are "Never Trumpers" believe that Trump is giving much needed medical supplies such as masks, gowns, and ventilators only to states with Republican governors. This theory was debunked when the governors of California and New York, both Democrats, praised Trump for sending not only supplies to their states but also for deploying the hospital ship **Mercy** to New York City. Educated people have become irrational. I have a well-educated cousin, also a Trump hater, who asked if Trump built the controversial wall on our southern border, how was the virus able to penetrate the wall and enter our country? Then there are the conservatives who ask, "If the Democrats hadn't been so obsessed with impeaching Trump for being beholden to Russia (which was later disproven) when the virus started spreading out of control in China, might they have had their eye on the ball and been better able to address the impending threat of the virus?" People are out of work, and children are forced to learn virtually at home via computer; New York City and Los Angeles look like ghost towns; everyone is afraid of being exposed to the deadly virus; children and adults are wearing masks and vinyl gloves. We are following the advice of President Trump's task force headed by Dr. Anthony Fauci and Dr. Debbie Birks, both of whom have dictated our behavior by establishing the protocol of social distancing, wearing masks, staying away from supermarkets and houses of worship, using hand sanitizers, and avoiding all social contact, including handshakes and hugs. Because so many people are out of work and stores, companies, and offices have been forced to close, the economy has tanked, and talks of a major recession, even a depression, are circulating.

* * *

May 30, 2020

    America is burning. Literally. In the midst of the corona-virus pandemic, there is now a new reason for discord and unrest. On May 25th, a white police officer in Minneapolis, Minnesota, murdered a black man by placing his entire body weight onto the man's neck with his knee. Two other officers held the man down, while a third stood by and watched. The perpetrator, George Floyd, had used a counterfeit $20 bill at a local bodega, and the police were called. He was apprehended without resistance, handcuffed and then, for no apparent reason, he was thrown to the ground where he was murdered. The video is horrific. This incident triggered massive riots not only on the streets of Minneapolis but in other cities across the country as well, including Los Angeles, Seattle, Portland, Atlanta, Washington D.C., Philadelphia, and New York City. The murder, along with the already tense and stressful state of the country because of the pandemic and its resultant shutdowns and massive unemployment, have created the perfect storm for an eruption that has led to the burning of cars, the destruction of buildings, the blowing up of ATM machines, unbridled violence against the police, storming of police stations, toppling of iconic statues like George Washington and Christoper Columbus, as well as vociferous demonstrations in front of the White House. The hatred and vitriol remain evident on Facebook, where I cringe every time I see the hateful rhetoric against President Trump, accusing him of instigating the deadly incident, despite the fact that he has openly denounced this murder and ordered the Justice Department to conduct a full investigation. Inter-estingly enough, the murderer/cop had several complaints against him. He had killed another person when Amy Klobuchar, a Democrat presidential candidate on the short-list to be named Biden's vice-presidential running mate, exonerated him when she was a prosecutor in Minnesota. Yet Trump is blamed!

* * *

June 12, 2020
My 54th Wedding Anniversary

> *The political divide deepens. The vitriol spouted by many of my liberal friends on Facebook has not subsided, and the equally hateful responses by my conservative friends have resurfaced. The rate of unemployment is at a record high, and the economy is in free fall. Protestors are demanding defunding the police, resulting in an historical, unbridled crime rate in major cities. Rioters have torn down statues of leaders they deem to be racist, including Jefferson Davis, who was the only president of the Confederate States of America and served as U.S. Secretary of War (1853-57), as well as iconic figures who had always been revered, such as George Washington, Abraham Lincoln, Thomas Jefferson, and Benjamin Franklin. Even poor Christopher Columbus has been beheaded!*
> *The country is going to hell in a handbasket.*

* * *

August 2, 2020

> *The pandemic has taken its toll in many ways far worse than the disease itself. People are depressed, out of work, and rightfully frustrated, manifesting their anger in vitriolic political rants that can only be described as psychotic. It is reported that there have been more deaths from suicide, drug use, alcoholism, and domestic violence than from the virus itself. Civil unrest has been sparked by the death of George Floyd at the hands of a police officer and inflamed by self-described anti-fascist terrorist groups such as Antifa, who have taken advantage of the legitimate demonstrations by infiltrating the peaceful protesters and unleashing death and destruction onto cities all around the country. Demands to defund police departments have resulted in exponential increases in crime with corresponding record numbers of murders, rapes, robberies, and burning*

and looting of business establishments. *Statues of iconic figures are being knocked down amid cheers and rantings by groups intent on bringing down not only these statues but also our country and society as we know it. God help us all!*

* * *

August 17, 2020

I experienced culture shock when I saw the sign on the bus flashing "Face Coverings Required" as it passed me during my first venture outside since the start of the pandemic. I soon realized that it is a sign of the times. The stark reality of the situation continued to sink in at the Xfinity Store, where I went to buy a new cell phone. There were round signs stuck onto the floor six feet apart, indicating to the customers that they must remain at a safe social distance from one another. All of the workers were wearing face masks, and plexiglass barriers separating the customers from the Xfinity employees had been erected. Three months ago, I never even heard of **Zoom***. Now, it is a household word, and I find myself signing onto* **Zoom** *for my Torah Studies class, my choir, my book club, my writing group, and* **House Party***, where we mingle and play games with our children and grandkids every Sunday night.*

It saddens me that the divisiveness of our nation has extended to personal relationships between family members. Children won't talk to their Trump-supporting parents. Brothers with opposing political views refuse to associate with one another. Best friends are on the outs. A close relative even hung up on me when we were discussing politics over the phone! It's crazy! Hopefully, our country will put aside its differences and come together.

Two

Casualties of the Pandemic

The Lockdown

lock·down: *the confining of prisoners to their cells, typically after an escape or to regain control during a riot; a state of isolation or restricted access instituted as a security measure.*

The word lockdown used to mean what happened to incarcerated prisoners, just like grass was the green stuff you mowed and gay meant happy. But the double entendre of the word has become woefully apparent in this era of the Pandemic of 2020. The lockdown will have far-reaching consequences that will still remain evident long after this septuagenarian is gone.

The COVID-19 pandemic has affected the entire world. Besides the devastating physical effects of the virus, including systemic debilitation, loss of the sense of smell and taste, extreme fatigue, respiratory distress, and even death, one of the most far-reaching and disastrous consequences have been the universal lockdowns that have been imposed on people and businesses all over the world.

Shortly after the virus first reared its ugly head, heads of government from China to Chicago, from Italy to Indianapolis, from New Delhi to New York, ordered the lockdown of restaurants, gyms, schools, stores, houses of worship, and any other venues where people gathered. The lockdowns were supposed to provide a temporary fix until the curve of acceleration of the deadly virus was flattened and the virus was under control. The fifteen-*day* lockdown imposed on March 16, 2020, to flatten the curve of the number of cases morphed into a twenty-one *month* imposition. Sweden, South Korea, Florida, South Dakota, Arizona, and Texas are among those few locations where lockdowns were lifted early on or were never imposed in the first place. It does not seem that they are any worse off than those areas where the lockdowns remained in place, and in many respects, they fared much better. Those places did not suffer the disastrous consequences such as increased rates of suicide, alcoholism, drug usage, child abuse, domestic violence, and depression to the same extent as places where lockdowns were strictly enforced.

Many of the students who have been forced to learn via computer from home have not even attended their virtual classes, placing them in a no-win situation. Not only have young people been deprived of their education, but their parents have been forced to give up their jobs in order to stay home with their school-age children, creating friction, animosity, and resentment, often leading to child abuse, anxiety, depression, and even suicide. One study reported that the rate of serious mental health issues has more than doubled in the United States during the pandemic. Millions of jobs have been lost as a result of the lockdowns. The elderly are dying from isolation and dementia, and the overall health of many people has been compromised because of fear to venture out for routine testing such as mammograms and colonoscopies.

In our zeal to thwart the devastating physical effects of the virus, have we thrown the baby away with the bathwater? Is the cure worse than the disease? Are we burning down the house to kill a rat?

* * *

Cancel Culture

The stress and divisiveness of the pandemic has given rise to a new phenomenon called "cancel culture," which is a modern form of ostracism in which someone is thrust out of social or professional circles, whether it be online, on social media, or in person. Political correctness has gone amok and has taken a dramatic leap. Employers who take issue with what someone said or even implied can, on a whim, declare that person undesirable and "cancel" him. Many such unsuspecting individuals have been fired from their jobs, shamed on social media, or forced to apologize for unintentional insults they may have uttered decades ago. Former Vice President Mike Pence's book deal was cancelled by Simon & Schuster, who also banned the works of anyone associated with the Trump Administration. Dr. Seuss' first book *And to Think That I Saw It on Mulberry Street* joined the trash heap, along with Disney's movies *Dumbo* (1941), *Peter Pan* (1953), *Swiss Family Robinson* (1960), and *The Aristocats* (1970). Stand-up comedians like Dave Chappelle have been cancelled from their gigs because of their politically incorrect jokes. Even our founding fathers have not escaped the chopping block, and schools honoring the great legacies of George Washington, Abraham Lincoln, Thomas Jefferson, and Ben Franklin are being renamed.

It seems that the stress of dealing with the pandemic has unleashed pent-up vitriol in many disgruntled people and given them license to destroy the reputations of those with whom they disagree. Everything is fair game to them, and they have no second thoughts or any qualms about how their criticism can ruin someone's livelihood and good name. Once a person has been cancelled, even if the accuser retracts his or her assertion, the accused can rightfully ask, "Where do I go to get my reputation back?"

* * *

Masked vs Unmasked

Vaxxed vs Unvaxxed

Another casualty of this pandemic is the difference of opinion between those who believe in the value of mask-wearing and those who don't, as well as those who are firm supporters of vaccines and serial booster shots and those who denounce their efficacy. Parents have become irate that their children are required to wear masks in school, where it has been reported that some teachers have actually taped masks onto children's faces. Anti-vaxxers are angry because mandates have been imposed upon them, making vaccinations prerequisites for job employment, travel, eating in restaurants, or enjoying a Broadway show. Rather than rewarding the nurses, doctors, EMS workers, police officers, and firefighters who put their lives on the line to care for those afflicted with the COVID-19 virus when the pandemic first emerged, bureaucracy has deemed it necessary to punish these brave men and women by taking away their livelihood and banning them from employment simply because they refuse to get vaccinated. Conversely, proponents of vaccinations and booster shots truly believe that their anti-vax counterparts are selfish and uncaring, even unpatriotic.

I can only hope that once the panic and hype over this virus settles down, those who disagree with each other will eventually become more rational and learn to tolerate opposing views.

* * *

Tarnished Silver Lining

The bloom is off the rose. Whatever silver lining we ascribed to the pandemic at its inception, such as greater productivity, fuller appreciation of life, love and respect of our fellow man, joining together to fight the common enemy (the virus), has become so tarnished that productivity is at a standstill, pessimism prevails, people are frustrated and more divided than ever before, and there is widespread disagreement about how to conquer the disease.

Many people believe that it is time to learn to live with this virus and resume our normal lives. Just as we have adjusted to the recurrent annual flu, it is time for us to deal with COVID-19 in a similar fashion. We must end the divisiveness, finger-pointing, and hatefulness toward those with different opinions. Being the eternal optimist, I feel confident that we will come together.

PART TEN

Moving Forward

One

Coping with Covid

When the world gives you lemons, make lemonade.
My cup is half full.
And this, too, shall pass.

We welcome the new year, 2022, not with hope and anticipation, but with continued fear and uncertainty. Our country, and indeed the entire world, is suffering from the effects of the coronavirus pandemic that has gripped our nation for the past two years. Wearing masks, lockdowns, severe punishment for the unvaccinated, and other draconian mandates have left our country in a very dark place. The pandemic may be the root cause of our uncertainty and unhappiness, but it is not the only culprit. Our nation's political divide, economic woes, cancel culture, class warfare, non-stop infighting between the masked and unmasked and the vaccinated and unvaccinated, all contribute to the pessimism and hopelessness so many of us are feeling. Republicans are disgruntled. Democrats are disappointed. College students have become disenfranchised. Blacks feel victimized because of their skin color, while Whites are persecuted and presumed to be racist simply because of their complexion. Women athletes believe that their sports have been hijacked by competing transgender males, and men feel emasculated by domineering women. Border patrol agents are demoralized, while the defunded and disrespected police have been demonized. The military feels abandoned and ineffectual. It is no wonder that our children are confused and dismayed. So, as I said before, our country is in a very dark place, which, according to urbandictionary.com, is the place a person finds himself after enduring an enormous disappointment or loss. This leads to an emotional funk with depression of unbearable proportion and an acute exaggerated feeling of anxiety, angst, or distress. There seems to be every reason to feel discouraged and disillusioned.

In a desperate effort to be positive and feel more optimistic, we have latched onto a litany of cliches: *When the world gives you lemons, make lemonade; My cup is half full; And this, too, shall pass.* Unfortunately, the coronavirus did not turn out to be the blessing in disguise that we optimistically envisioned. All of the potentially positive side effects we tried to attribute to the pandemic have worn thin, and people have stopped rationalizing that anything good has come from it.

But our country has faced dark times before, and it has managed to rally and come back stronger. We survived the Civil War, two world wars, the Great Depression, the 1918 Spanish flu pandemic, and the polio and tuberculosis epidemics. The American people are a strong and optimistic lot, and through strength, courage, and perseverance, we have always found the wherewithal to get through these almost impossible challenges. The Civil War led to Reconstruction, the Emancipation Proclamation, and the termination of one of our country's most shameful eras. The Pandemic of 1918 gave us insight into the spread of germs and taught us the importance of social distancing, wearing masks, and hand washing. And World War II spawned one of the greatest eras of economic expansion in world history.

The Pollyanna in me is convinced that these cliches are not merely cliches. Hope springs eternal, and I am confident that, yes, when the world gives you lemons, make lemonade; my cup is indeed half full; and this, too, shall pass. So I have decided to conclude this book of vignettes on a positive note with the final chapter, "On Optimism."

Two

On Optimism

*"In spite of everything
I still believe that people are really good at heart."*
Anne Frank

There is a parable about identical twins who were opposite in every way. One was an eternal optimist, and the other was a confirmed pessimist. On the day of their birthday, their father loaded the pessimist's room with every imaginable toy and game, while he filled the optimist's room with horse manure.

When the father passed by the pessimist's room, he found the child sitting amid his new gifts crying bitterly, complaining about the complicated instructions of the games and bemoaning the fear that all of his new toys would eventually break.

Passing the optimistic twin's room, the father saw him with a shovel in his hands digging feverishly, all the while exclaiming, "With all of this horse shit, there's got to be a pony in here somewhere!"

In her eighth-grade autograph album, my mother Rosie stated that her favorite book was *The Lamplighter*. Written in 1854 by Maria Susanna Cummins, it tells the story of a young girl named Gertrude Flint, an abandoned and mistreated orphan who, at the age of eight, is rescued from her abusive guardian by a lamplighter named Truman Flint. In this coming-of-age novel, Gertrude is a hopeless optimist, always finding the good in people and in life itself. I wonder whether Rosie was drawn to this book because of her already unwavering optimism or if her lifelong optimism was a result of having read the book as a young girl. Whatever the reason, Rosie was definitely an optimist, putting a positive spin on events and people she encountered throughout her life. I am convinced that Rosie's longevity can be attributed to her unwavering optimism despite the many physical challenges she faced.

Similarly, I have always been drawn to another book called *Pollyanna* by Eleanor H. Porter. Like Gertrude in *The Lamplighter*, Pollyanna Whittier is an orphan, and despite being exposed to many negative encounters, including an abusive guardian aunt, her primary goal in life is to find happiness and see the good in people. She indulges in playing "the glad game," in which the goal is to "find something about everything to be glad about," whether it's a disappointing Christmas gift or a serious illness. Pollyanna uses the game to spread good cheer among townspeople, including a self-pitying invalid, a grouchy old miser, a poor orphan, and a preacher. The book was published in 1913 (the year Rosie was born), and although Rosie did not cite it as her favorite book, my guess is that she not only read it but that it also reinforced her already optimistic and positive attitude toward life.

I know that it took a great deal of effort for Rosie to remain optimistic and stoic throughout her life in spite of her chronic continual pain and illness. It is easy to be positive when things are

going your way. In *The Lamplighter*, Maria Susanna Cummins sums
it up like this:

"There is no merit in being patient and good-tempered when
there is nothing to irritate you."

* * *

In her book, *The Choice*, Dr. Edith Eva Egers, a ninety-four-year-
old Holocaust survivor with a PhD in psychology, asserts that even
though bad things will inevitably befall every one of us, it is how
we respond to them that is of primary importance. Either we can
become **victims** of our circumstances or we can become **survivors.**
The choice is ours.

* * *

Shakespeare's Hamlet reflects on how we view adversity when
he muses, "There is nothing either good or bad, but thinking makes
it so." And Abraham Lincoln reminded us that "People are about as
happy as they make up their minds to be."

As this book of reflections draws to a close, I would like to im-
part upon you, my readers, the importance of remaining optimistic
in the chaotic, seemingly hopeless state in which we find ourselves.
During an earlier period of social and racial unrest, Martin Luther
King, Jr. encouraged us to move ahead by declaring that "we shall
overcome." And as the optimist in the story of the twins so hopefully exclaimed, "With all this horse shit, there must be a pony here
somewhere!"

Acknowledgments

UNASSUMING HEROES

When we hear about a young person assisting a senior citizen, we conjure up a picture of a Boy Scout helping a little old lady cross a busy street or a kindly young Good Samaritan carrying groceries up to her elderly neighbor's third-floor walk-up apartment. Fortunately, I can cross the street myself, and I have no problem carrying my groceries on my own. I had a very different positive experience with four young people who helped me in achieving a lifelong endeavor.

For several years, I talked about publishing a memoir but didn't know how to go about it. The idea of publishing a book was so daunting that I suffered from what psychologists call approach-avoidance conflict. I really *wanted* to publish a book, but my fear led to complete inertia and *prevented* me from moving forward.

Then I met Stefani Milan, my guardian angel sent to me in order to fulfill a dream that I had been carrying around for decades. Stefani's kindness, encouragement, and insight did not end with the publication of my first memoir, **Rosie (and me)**. My angel followed me as I embarked on the journey to write this second memoir, **Vignettes on Life: Reflections of a Septuagenarian**.

Stefani is a strong believer in cosmic synergy. She believes that it was destined for us to meet. Both our mothers' names were Rose, and they shared the same birthday. Although I am somewhat of a skeptic, I must admit that I agree with Stefani. I am so lucky that our paths were meant to cross.

Anyone who doubts that a religious person can also be a creative writer, has not met my son, Todd (Chaim). He gave me the great idea for the opening wedding scene introducing all of the characters in my first memoir, *Rosie (and me)*. When he was a young boy, he used to balk when I corrected his school reports and even complained to his grandmother, "Why did my Mom have to be an English teacher?" I'm happy that I instilled in him the love of writing. He became a talented writer, who has the ability to critique the works of others in a constructive manner. He has certainly paid me back for all of the effort I put into his writing with his peer feedback and insightful suggestions.

* * *

My son Jeff is the very essence of a middle child. As far back as second grade, his teacher, Mrs. Gray, described him as a boy who "marches to the drum of his own band!"

When I decided to narrate *Rosie (and me)* so that it would be available as an audiobook, Jeff packed up his fancy sound equipment and high-end microphone and brought them from Los Angeles to Cherry Hill, where he set up a recording studio in my walk-in closet and began the arduous task of recording my long-awaited memoir. We recorded into the wee hours of the night, and Jeff did not hesitate to chide me for using my voice too much during the day or starting too late at night, resulting in a raspy, tired sound to my otherwise smooth and vibrant voice. A month later, we met in Las Vegas to resume pick-ups with parts of the recording that still needed work. He chastised me when I had uncontrollable, barely noticeable, quiet burps that came from nowhere but were picked up by Jeff's expensive sound-sensitive equipment. It was such fun recording the book with Jeff as my director, sound guy, and recording studio guru. He made me record so many takes that I threatened to report him to the authorities for elder abuse! His perseverance and attention to detail resulted in *Rosie (and me)* becoming an audiobook. When all is said and done, Jeff continues to be a firm supporter of my writing, encouraging his septuagenarian mother to pursue her dreams.

* * *

My daughter Emily was a successful book editor, who came out of retirement to edit *Vignettes on Life: Reflections of a Septuagenarian*. Her expert detail-oriented editing enhanced my manuscript, and I am forever grateful to her for doing this. My guess is that she learned a lot that she did not know about her mother after reading and editing *Vignettes on Life*.

One of the perks of getting old is becoming a friend and a professional partner with your adult children. I am delighted that I have achieved this relationship not only with Emily, but with all three of my children.

So I give thanks to these young people who were willing to take the time and effort to help this septuagenarian realize her dream. None wore a scout uniform or dressed in a candy-striper outfit. Each, in his or her own unique way, held my hand, not to cross the street or carry my groceries, but to walk me through the "slings and arrows" that I faced as an aspiring new writer. I am forever grateful to Stefani, Todd, Jeff, and Emily - my unassuming heroes.

STEVE

"The most important person in your life is your mate."

Rose Anderman

My partner in life is also my soulmate, my lover, my mentor, my editor, my compass, my pillar, my greatest fan, and unwavering supporter of my writing endeavors. A take-charge person, there was never a time when he hasn't been there with me and for me. As a freshman in medical school, when my cousin was dying in a small hospital on Long Island, Steve arranged for her to be transferred to Flower Fifth Avenue Hospital where she underwent emergency surgery. This act of courage saved her life. When my father, who was suffering from acute leukemia, could no longer get blood that was compatible with his own, essential for the transfusions to keep him alive, Steve found a laboratory in Pennsylvania that could provide custom-made blood that my father needed. This was in 1984, long before computers were available to facilitate locating such a lab. Even the oncologist marveled at this incredible feat, stating that Steve was always three steps ahead of him.

In times of need and decision-making, Steve was always the one called upon, whether it was arranging for my mother's pacemaker, informing my father of his terminal illness, calling in specialists when his mother had a heart attack, even answering the telephone when it rang in the middle of the night because I was fearful that one of our parents might be calling with an emergency or terrible news. He is tough when he needs to be, but underneath the toughness is a soft, tender, and sensitive man. The pride he has for his children and in everything they do, his love of nature, of flowers and trees and birds and animals, often alien to a boy who grew up in the Bronx (or "Da Bronks" as he likes to say!) exemplify his sensitivity. He has an intense involvement with his children's interests, whether it is Emily's editing career, Todd's Torah studies, or Jeffrey's movie. He never tires of his conversations with them, and he has an unending ability to listen to their ideas and problems, even when he is tired and laden with his own.

Among other things, he has been the most careful and constructively critical editor of my writing, offering me suggestions and insights that I would never have thought of on my own. He never fails to promote my book, and if you ever find yourself in a conversation with him, don't expect to get away before he tells you what a great book *Rosie (and me)* is!

Afterward

Despite the negative experience I had when I took a workshop in memoir writing decades ago, I decided to register for an online writing workshop with Dani Shapiro who wrote *Still Writing: The Perils and Pleasures of a Creative Life.* One of the exercises of the class was to write a short essay entitled, "Five Years From Now Looking Back." This is what I wrote in 2021:

Talk about the road not taken! Going back five years, I see that I am almost finished with my second memoir, **Vignettes on Life: Reflections of a Septuagenarian.** *I am seventy-six years old, and I am determined to publish this memoir before my next birthday, when I will be nudging my eightieth birthday. If I wait too long, I will have to change the title. I would hate to do that, as the word* septuagenarian *has a much better ring to it than* octogenarian! *Am I regretful that I didn't follow through? Or am I grateful that I persevered and published the book?*

The answers to these questions are clear. You have just finished reading **Vignettes on Life: Reflections of a Septuagenarian.**

Addendum

WHAT SIMON WROTE

INTRODUCTION

The first time I typed these essays was in 1963 during my father's first semester as a college student at Rockland Community College where he was enrolled in a Freshman English composition class. He was fifty-three years old, and I was a nineteen-year-old sophomore at City College in New York. With him sitting alongside me at the kitchen table in our house in Spring Valley, I deciphered his handwritten notes and typed them on my manual Smith Corona typewriter. There was no computer, no word processor, not even an electric typewriter!

In a span of just four months, he produced a plethora of essays that were not only descriptive, but insightful and poetic as well. I can only imagine what he might have accomplished had he devoted a lifetime to his writing. I have no doubt that he would have stood with other great writers to whom I previously alluded.

I am so happy that I kept his compositions and still have them sixty years later. I have retyped them on my Apple MacPro laptop computer exactly as he wrote them six decades ago; and I am thrilled to be introducing his writings to whomever may read this humble memoir. I guarantee that you are in for a real treat!

Simon Anderman
English 101
Professor Mitchell
September 24, 1963

MY GOALS

The longer I confronted the title of the assignment, the greater was my dismay. It had been so long since I had given thought to my goals in life. If the question had been posed years ago, when I was still attending high school, my answer would undoubtedly have been glib: Make a lot of money, live a life of adventure, have a good time. Had I been asked my aim in life several years later, during the days of the Great Depression, my answer then would have been terse, imploring and more to the point: A job, with wages. The experiences of those days, the hardships, frustrations, and uncertainties left indelible impressions. I doubt if those who have lived through them can ever really lose sight of the value of material advantages. The dignity attaching to a life comparatively free from want, independent and self-sufficient is a priceless commodity.

Fortunately, present conditions are vastly different. Thanks to the enlightened leadership of Franklin Roosevelt, who blazed the path to our economic well-being with his program of social and economic reform, we Americans are no longer so acutely faced with such problems. The satisfaction of our wants is more easily achieved. Several years ago, I was fortunate enough to be able to change my occupation. From a work day of about ten hours, my present position requires less than forty hours of work each week. With this improvement in my economic situation and the lessening of the time required to earn my livelihood, my thoughts turned to the idea of completing my formal education. I must confess that I toyed with this idea for some time, took no steps to start, and it was only the urgings and encouragement given me by my wife that caused me to enroll in this school.

It is difficult for me to state what my specific goal is at this stage of my life. A goal implies a point one intends to reach in the future, either by accomplishment or by acquisition. My goal and my wishes and hopes for the future are intermingled and entwined so that it is difficult to identify one from the other. By continuing my education, I hope to broaden my capacity to enjoy the finer things of life and our cultural heritage. I also want to achieve a more philosophical outlook toward life, develop a greater capacity to understand people. Above all, the well-being of those close to me is paramount. My goals and wishes seem to be a rather large order, and I will be thankful for some measure of fulfillment.

Simon Anderman
English 101
Professor Mitchell
October 8, 1963

AUTUMN SCENE

The soft caressing browns and deep reds of the foliage bordering the dwelling were a reminder that autumn had arrived and that time was sliding swiftly along to the year's end. The thick layer of fallen leaves covered the ground as would a soft carpet, hiding the unkempt appearance of the lawn. Nature, with her incessant recreation of plant life, seemed to have made an attempt to shield the old dwelling from the prying eyes of pedestrians and passing motorists. However, as the shrubbery was denuded and the trees became naked and bare, the forlorn house was exposed in all its shabbiness, its door boarded up, abandoned and forsaken by the ones whom it once used to shelter and protect.

I had passed this old home frequently for many months without seeing it, until one day, while walking by, a scampering squirrel on the steps of the building caught my attention. It was late spring, and the golden dandelions were beginning to show on the surrounding lawn, crowding out the lingering wild violets and buttercups. A first meeting with a deserted house is a depressing experience, even if it is in the spring with her promise of Nature's coming gifts. It was early evening, and having finished my day's work, I had time to stand for a while and observe the old structure. Other than the fleeing squirrel, there was no sign of life, but the steps leading to the entrance door were rounded and worn, a mute reminder of the goings and comings of former occupants. Although unpainted and with gaping holes where window panes had long ago been broken out by the unerring aim of rock-throwing boys, the building looked remarkably sturdy. Why, I thought had its former masters, whom the house had served so long and so well, left it, uncared for and defenseless?

The scene saddened me. I wondered who had first proudly called this his home, and what events had transpired between then and the final desertion of the dwelling. Day-dreaming is not difficult in the spring, and as I stood there, I pictured the many happy occasions that the house had witnessed - the happy coming of children, their joyous laughter, and the other deep pleasures of life which undoubtedly were all too fleeting. I thought also of the troubles that the house had seen in the many years that it had given shelter and warmth to its tenants, until the time when the very last person had departed. Is this why the house seemed so unbearably sad? Did it deserve to have been left to stand so wretchedly alone?

My day-dream faded. Perhaps my thoughts had been in-spired by a subconscious feeling of dread that I might someday suffer a like fate. Whatever the reason, my feelings were relieved by the beauty of the spring scene.

As I walked away, I thought that a deserted home should be destroyed, not because it is ugly, but because it is so pathetically friendless and unloved.

Simon Anderman
English 101
Mr. Mitchell
November 5, 1963

VANITY

The human animal differs in many ways from the other creatures that inhabit the earth. We are acquisitive far beyond our immediate needs; we covet our neighbor's possessions and will scheme to take them from him. Sometimes we are kind, generous, and unselfish as we were taught to be when we were children. We can also laugh either good-naturedly or in a derisive, unkindly fashion. For most of our lives, we are blindly optimistic, sure that we will come out on top and that bad things cannot happen to us, only to the other fellow. One other very basic universal trait we all possess is vanity. Most of us think we are unique, more attractive, smarter, and with a brighter future than other people. A cross-country trip I once took gave me a better perspective on life and rid me of most of my feelings of self-importance.

Several years ago, my family and I went on an automobile trip to California. This was to be our first chance to see our great land's marvelous scenery between New York and the West Coast. The Blue Ridge Mountains, the Ozarks, and the Mississippi River were all very interesting sights, as were the oil fields of Oklahoma and the Texas cattle country. The towering Rockies, the magnificent California countryside, and the beautiful Pacific Ocean were also very impressive. On the whole trip, however, the most awe-inspiring and stupendous experience was to see the Grand

Canyon. It was a scene that made me think and realize that my personal desires, my plans and ambitions were really not of world-shaking importance. Looking down into the Grand Canyon and over the great chasm was an experience I will never forget. The erosive action of wind, weather, and the rushing river has carved out a cleft that seems to reach the center of the earth. The vari-shaded colors of the rocks, earth, and vegetation are magnificent, and the high skies over the deep Canyon are indescribably beautiful. The magnitude of nature and her irresistible power is overwhelming. It made me feel small and insignificant. As I stood there, I remembered that a friend had once told me that if all the people in all the world were to be cremated, they would make only a small pile of ashes in a corner of the Grand Canyon.

The lesson I learned from this has never left my mind. It has helped me see things a little more clearly because now I realize that the problems that beset us are not too significant. Only yesterday, this feeling was emphasized when I read in the New York Times that every time one of us celebrates his birthday, there are nine million others doing the same thing throughout the world.

It is funny, however, that this morning I still shaved carefully, looked in the mirror, and used my favorite Old Spice After Shave Lotion. Vanity!

Simon Anderman
English 101
Mr. Mitchell
October 15, 1963

VIGIL

The large clock dominated the entire area. From its position on the wall facing the entrance, it stared at the almost deserted hospital lobby. The walls were painted a light gray, and the floor was covered with tiles arranged in a monotonous pattern, running to the black border along the base of the wall. To the right of the street door was a counter, behind which was the hospital office, furnished with desks and filing cabinets. A woman sitting at the telephone switchboard was the only worker in attendance. It was a lonely scene.

In the section of the lobby reserved for visitors, a small group of people occupied a couch and one easy chair. There were four: a teen-age girl, a young man in his twenties, and an older man and woman. They had been sitting there for a long time, speaking infrequently and then in the hushed, low voices generally used in hospitals. It had been midnight when they first arrived, escorting a fifth person, a young woman who had been quickly taken by a nurse to the waiting elevator. The group had been waiting anxiously ever since, fidgeting nervously and obviously worried. Their eyes seemed to be constantly turning to the clock. The older woman asked frequently why they weren't told anything, but no one answered. It seemed to them that they had been there for an endless period, yet it was less than three hours since they had arrived. Whenever the elevator door opened, they expectantly looked up, but the doctor or nurse that emerged usually did not even glance toward them The teen-ager, exhausted, dozed on the chair.

A young man came through the door from the street and walked quickly to the seated people, asking loudly, "How is she? Why are you all sitting here? I came home and the house was deserted. I didn't know what to think until I saw your note on the table." In low tones, they told him that they didn't know, they were waiting, too worried to leave. From the conversation, it was apparent that the newcomer was a brother of the hospitalized woman. When told how long they had been there, he, too, sat down despondently. The older woman looked again at the clock and announced that she just couldn't stand the strain any longer. The young man in his twenties who was the husband of the woman who had been admitted as a patient gently tried to calm her. His voice sounded as if he was trying to ease his own fears. Before he could say much more, the elevator door opened again. A nurse strode out, the one who had taken the young woman up so long ago. The entire group seemed to get to its feet in unison and surrounded the nurse. She smiled and announced loudly, "It's a six-pound boy." The young man embraced her. They were all so glad. The clock, with its hands at a quarter to three, seemed to be smiling at the happy family. Their vigil was over.

Simon Anderman
English 101
Mr. Mitchell
October 29, 1963

DEADLY WEAPON

An instrument used to destroy life is called a deadly weapon. It is not always something the killer carries hidden in his pocket. It has many forms and shapes. A gun, a knife, or a club can be used. Many times even an automobile becomes a deadly weapon.

About two years ago, during the Christmas holiday season, a news item in the local press gave an account of an automobile accident which had caused the death of a young man. Unfortunately, fatalities resulting from the careless use of automobiles are all too frequent. If the victim or the other people involved are strangers, the account is just another statistic, almost meaningless to the casual reader. In this case, the name of the survivor, the operator of one of the cars, was familiar to me. He was an old acquaintance - someone I had known for several years, and the details of the accident were, therefore, of particular interest to me.

The two men had been co-workers, friendly towards each other. The day of the accident there had been a party to celebrate the holiday, and the two left early after exchanging good wishes with those remaining. Neither man seemed to be intoxicated. Each got into his own car and drove off. Less than five minutes later, the younger of the two men had crashed head-on into an oncoming car and had been killed instantly. Subsequent investigation by the police and the testimony of two eye-witnesses resulted in the arrest of my friend. The witnesses, a couple driving behind the two men, had charged that the two drivers had been drag-racing. The survivor denied this, claiming that the dead man had tried to pass him and that this was the reason for the fatal accident. The jurors believed the witnesses, and my friend was convicted of culpable negligence resulting in vehicular homicide. He was sentenced to serve a year in Sing-Sing Prison.

After his release, I happened to meet my friend, and he repeated his claims of innocence. At this time, of course, the issue was academic. One man was dead, and the other had lost a year of his life. What actually happened that fatal day is known only to my friend. Did he mean to destroy his co-worker? Was his action deliberate and intentional? Only he can answer these questions.

This tragic incident brought to my mind a thought that had often occurred to me. The advertising men who glamorize the products of Detroit use very fancy words to entice customers. They tell the American motorist that if he will buy this year's model, his status will grow and he will be envied by all his neighbors. The cars are described as being sleek, sporty, rich looking, and glamorous. The adjectives used to attract customers are numerous and varied, but one thing they fail to do is to warn buyers that their purchase is potentially a deadly weapon.

Simon Anderman
English 101
Mr. Mitchell
October 1, 1963

CHARACTER SKETCH

One cannot refute the logic of the person who first said that human beings are the greatest of all enigmas. Especially in modern society, where some people are exposed to so many and so varied experiences, a person is apt to develop numerous contradictory characteristics. A kindly person may occasionally be inconsiderate and cruel, an intelligent person may make a foolish remark, and conversely, a fool may say something profoundly wise, and an evil man may do a good deed.

One of the friendliest, most kindly people I know is one such complex individual. Let me hasten to add that I find no evil in this man, who is one of my co-workers. He takes a keen interest in his work and applies himself industriously. He would like to advance to a position of more authority, but his eccentric dress and his outspoken speech thwart this ambition. He does not hesitate to reveal the details of his modest way of life and to discuss the condition of his third-rate apartment. He has a phobia about people living in modern housing developments which have units selling for large sums. How can we rationalize this attitude and his standard of living with the fact that people in his occupation with similar responsibilities live in greater comfort and in more desirable quarters? He has a sharp tongue, ready to point out and ridicule a mispronounced word, an improperly accented syllable, yet a remark directed to him, pointing out a real short-coming, will offend him. When he takes the initiative in a conversation, he will make himself the butt of belittling remarks, displaying a resignation to what he believes to be his unfortunate situation. Still, most times he is considerate, extremely helpful, and will accept criticism of his work without resentment. May I add that he is the essence of integrity with respect to his work.

If my description is accused of being contradictory, I will be the first to admit to this fault. In a few short sentences I have tried to describe a person, the product of his environment, whose behavior reflects the experiences of his life. He is kind. He is mean. He is meek, and he is aggressive. He is considerate, and he is sharp. His traits may be likened to the diverse angles cut into a gem, its dull, ugly sides and those that reflect great beauty and color. I guess I will have to come back to my initial sentence. He is human, and as such, is an enigma.

Suggested Reading

Anderman, Pesach, **The Power of Life: Becoming a Human Being** (2012)

Bartov, Omer, **Anatomy of a Genocide: The Life and Death of a Town Called Buczacz** (2018)

Benisch, Pearl, **To Vanquish the Dragon** (1991)

Cummins, Maria Susanna, **The Lamplighter** (1854)

Egers, Edith Eva, **The Choice** (2018)

Golinkin, Lev, **A Backpack, A Bear, and Eight Crates of Vodka** (2014)

Harkavy, Carol, **Rosie (and me) - a memoir** (2017)

Keller, Helen, **Three Days to See** (essay) - (1933)

Porter, Eleanor H., **Pollyanna** (1913)

Saidel, Rochelle G., **Mielec, Poland: The Shtetl That Became a Nazi Concentration Camp** (2012)

ABOUT THE AUTHOR

Carol Harkavy is a firm believer that it is never too late to follow your dreams. In a span of almost eighty years, she has worn many hats - a mother, a wife, a college professor, a medical office manager, and finally, a published author. After perusing several volumes of personal journal entries, Carol Harkavy found herself in the unique position to objectively look back on her life and reflect upon what she did and how she might have done things differently. Through the eyes of a septuagenarian, she has compiled this collection of vignettes, offering lessons in life that she has gleaned over the past seven decades. She lives in New Jersey with her husband of fifty-seven years.

Printed in the USA
CPSIA information can be obtained
at www.ICGtesting.com
JSHW022049100923
47897JS00007B/11